Most 'defenders' of Levinas have undercut his genius by presenting him either as a pious old finger-wagging grandpa or as Jacques Derrida's halfhearted apprentice. In this book Tom Sparrow gives us the true Levinas: a formidable metaphysician who did more than anyone else to sensualize and concretize the work of Heidegger. Levinas is not in our rearview mirror, but remains in our motorcade today. He will still have much to teach us. Sparrow lucidly reminds us why.

Graham Harman, Associate Provost for Research Administration and Professor of Philosophy, American University in Cairo

Levinas Unhinged shows us another side of Levinas that is often ignored or overlooked. Sparrow's Levinas is foremost a philosopher of the night, attuned to the shadowy underbelly of appearances. Removed from his role as the high priest of ethics, Levinas appears in a new way. Now, the terms horror, indifference, and facelessness all come to the foreground as central to an understanding of Levinasian philosophy. This provocative reading is thus not only a challenge to Levinas scholarship, it is also a challenge to materialist ontology more broadly. The result is a worthy contribution to current debates in speculative realism and phenomenology.

Dylan Trigg, Research Fellow at École Normale Supérieure and University College Dublin

Levinas
Unhinged

Levinas Unhinged

Tom Sparrow

Winchester, UK
Washington, USA

First published by Zero Books, 2013
Zero Books is an imprint of John Hunt Publishing Ltd., Laurel House, Station Approach,
Alresford, Hants, SO24 9JH, UK
office1@jhpbooks.net
www.johnhuntpublishing.com
www.zero-books.net

For distributor details and how to order please visit the 'Ordering' section on our website.

Text copyright: Tom Sparrow 2012

ISBN: 978 1 78279 056 3

A CIP catalogue record for this book is available from the British Library.

Design: Stuart Davies

Printed and bound by CPI Group (UK) Ltd, Croydon, CR0 4YY

We operate a distinctive and ethical publishing philosophy in all
areas of our business, from our global network of authors to
production and worldwide distribution.

CONTENTS

For Graham Harman

The night stared me in the face, amorphous, blind, infinite, without frontiers.
— Stanislaw Lem, from *Solaris*

The darkness immersed everything; there was no hope of passing through its shadows, but one penetrated its reality in a relationship of overwhelming intimacy. [Thomas's] first observation was that he could still use his body, and particularly his eyes; it was not that he saw anything, but what he looked at eventually placed him in contact with a nocturnal mass which he vaguely perceived to be himself and in which he was bathed.
— Maurice Blanchot, from *Thomas the Obscure*

Haunting Levinas

Emmanuel Levinas is a haunting figure. Inside his texts, too, there are ghosts.

For a while now I have wanted to write a book that would display some of the underappreciated dimensions of Levinas's philosophy. This book would focus specifically on aspects not necessarily ethical in nature, but metaphysical instead; it would emphasize the dimension of materiality that accompanies, and in some respect grounds, his ethics. When taken as more fundamental to Levinas's project than the ethical, the dimension of materiality presents Levinas in a light radically different from that which illuminates his popular reception. Some may see this as darkening his image. While not untrue, such a view—typically expressed with a hint of reproach—misses the mark. I have assembled *Levinas Unhinged* to explain why. One recent day I realized that I had written several interrelated essays—which is to say, a book—on Levinas's philosophy. You are now reading that book. Its purpose is to exhibit what might be called a proto-materialist metaphysics leaking through the cracks of the familiar portrait of Levinas as a philosopher of transcendence. It resists the well-worn view that the Levinasian problematic is primarily, if not exclusively, ethical or theological in nature. The singular claim uniting the following chapters is that Levinas provides us with a speculative metaphysics and aesthetics which foregrounds the following: the body in its materiality; the irreducibility of aesthetic experience; the transcendental function of sensation; the ecological aspect of sensibility; the horror of existence. Levinas surprisingly keeps pace on occasion with philosophers of immanence like Gilles Deleuze. Therefore, what you find in these pages is a heterodox (perhaps heretical) and markedly non-phenomenological approach to Levinas's philosophy, one that features his insistence that subjectivity is nourished by the aesthetic environment, that is to say, the matter of sensation.

Adherents of Levinas's philosophy are notoriously protective of their master thinker, just as career Heideggerians often come off as dismissive of any commentary or criticism that does not issue from the inner circle of Heidegger scholarship. At times this adherence verges on religious piety, an attitude which really has no place in philosophy. Criticism of Levinas is often rebuffed as contrary to the spirit of Levinasian hospitality, as if highlighting the tone of an argument were enough to disarm its critical strength. Failure to enter the Levinasian problematic as Levinas understood it is seen as a failure to engage legitimately with the thinker, as if reading Levinas against his self-interpretation necessarily entails getting him wrong. It is perplexing that after the deconstructive revolution in reading, which for so long dominated the continental philosophy scene, this rebuttal carries as much weight as it does. It is doubly perplexing given that Levinas is often regarded as a principal ally of Jacques Derrida. As a reader of Levinas who places his ontology before his ethics, I read him otherwise than many of his commentators would have him read and perhaps otherwise than he would like to be read. This may be seen as an act of impiety, but whether or not it is heresy is irrelevant to the productivity of my reading. I am not trying to "get Levinas right" or advance his ethical program as it is typically understood. What I hope to have accomplished here is an account of Levinas as someone obsessed with matters besides God, the face of the Other, radical alterity, transcendence, and the usual Levinas catchwords. This is necessary, I think, because there are enough readers out there who believe that Levinas is little more than a quasi-religious thinker whose biggest contribution to philosophy is made as a member of the so-called theological turn in phenomenology denounced by

Dominique Janicaud; others see him as a forerunner of Derridean deconstruction. I make little attempt to engage either of these readings here. With any luck this book will end up enticing some of the uninitiated into Levinas's philosophy so that its metaphysical potential can be fully exploited.

The most familiar approach to Levinas obliges us to pass through his unique attempt to establish ethics as first philosophy. Nearly as influential is the reading of Levinas as a philosopher of difference or radical otherness. Additionally, he is seen as an undeniably central figure in the phenomenological movement (or as merely a phenomenologist, depending on your sympathies), as well as a Talmudic scholar. His contributions to political and environmental philosophy have inspired monographs and edited collections, but to a lesser extent and only recently. In the text that follows I present Levinas as first and foremost an engineer of ontology, as someone explicitly engaged in the establishment of a materialist account of subjectivity. At its most general level this book is about Levinas's sustained attention to the tangibility of being and the corporeal dimension of human existence. As I have already admitted, this is a deviant way of casting Levinas's project because it explicitly disregards the interpretation of his work that he and his faithful commentators provide. It does not keep with the spirit of Levinas. Nevertheless, my portrayal is grounded in evidence from the letter of his texts; this evidence is documented in the notes that close each chapter. The ontology I present is generated by Levinas's forays into phenomenology, especially the concepts of intentionality, representation, sensation, embodiment, and affectivity, but it entails a radical rethinking of the nature of subjectivity, the constitution of the environment, and the relationship between body and world. This radicalization takes place when subjectivity and environment are refracted through the lens of sensibility. At the end of the day Levinas's philosophy can be read (as I have here) as a concerted "rehabilitation of the sensible," as he himself would say. Sensation and sensibility, I argue, are concepts just as important to Levinas as the Other, the face, God, infinity, transcendence, or discourse.

Given the significance of sensation in Levinas's ontology it is time we read him as a philosopher of aesthetics as customarily as we read him as a philosopher of ethics. Each of the chapters that follow engage the aesthetic dimension of Levinasian philosophy, with the collective effect of raising the question: *Isn't aesthetics first philosophy for Levinas?* The question was first posed by Graham Harman in an essay titled "Aesthetics as First Philosophy: Levinas and the Non-Human," which appeared in the contemporary art and theory magazine *Naked Punch*.[1] Instead of pursuing the depths of individual substance in Levinas's ontology as Harman does, my investigations remain at the level of what he calls "enjoyment along the shallowest facades of the world." This is not to say that my attention is fixed on the phenomenal world, the world of appearances. What I am after, following Levinas, is the immanent reality the aesthetic harbors along its surfaces. To speak of the surfaces of things is also to speak of the source of sensation, the material currency of aesthetics. And to speak of enjoyment is to speak of the way in which sensation affects the body, folds back upon itself, and generates subjectivity.

This book is an assemblage of reworked conference papers, unpublished essays, and a couple of previously published articles. In addition to their critical commentary and productive engagement with Levinasian metaphysics, the chapters also touch upon themes in philosophical ecology, philosophy of race, philosophy of the body, and philosophy of art and architecture. The first three chapters provide strategic readings of Levinas's texts in order to foreground his attention to aesthetics and develop a sense of the materiality of his metaphysics. The fourth and fifth chapters apply this metaphysics to social and ethical issues to see what kind of practical work the heterodox reading of Levinas can do. The final chapter shows how Levinas's metaphysics of the subject evolves in the work of Alphonso Lingis, Levinas's translator and one of the most startling American philosophers of the twentieth and twenty-first centuries.

Chapter 1 introduces the theme of the night (pursued also in the second chapter) and shows in some detail how Levinas's discourse on the night contests the privileging of light and illumination in the Western philosophical tradition. In addition to offering a counterpoint to the pervasive metaphorics of light in Plato, Descartes, and Heidegger, Levinas's thinking of the night contributes to the history of ontology and the philosophy of embodiment. These two lines converge on the question of how the night figures into the adventure of subjectivity.

Chapter 2 looks at the function of sensation in Levinas's aesthetics and argues that sensation is for him the most basic element of experience. His metaphysics of sensation is remarkably similar to Deleuze's, so it is instructive, even if unorthodox, to read them side-by-side. Both thinkers defend a non-phenomenological logic of sensation that finds sensation at work behind the scenes of representation and below the level of perception and cognition. Any engagement with sensation entails a descent into the nocturnal anonymity of being and a confrontation with the rhythm of the sensible. While in one respect terrifying, this descent reveals itself to be crucial to the aesthetic edification of the subject.

Chapter 3 injects Levinas's thinking about sensation into discussion about the link between the body and its aesthetic environment. As embodied our identities are necessarily dependent on their natural and built surroundings. Maurice Merleau-Ponty's phenomenology deals with this idea at length; his work is enlisted by some architecture theorists who see phenomenology as a productive approach to their discipline. When read alongside this line of research, Levinas proves to be a useful tool for conceiving the materiality of the body/environment relation. But it is not his phenomenology that is instructive; it is his ontology of individuation. Phenomenology, I contend, must be abandoned in favor of an ontology that sees corporeal identity as generated by the materiality of aesthetic relations. Such an ontology is available in the work of figures like Deleuze and Spinoza, both of whom break down the natural/artificial and human/nonhuman distinctions. Levinas too contributes to this effort. Together they engender an environmental ethics grounded in the immanence of aesthetic relations and the plasticity of identity.

Chapter 4 looks at what Timothy Morton would call the "dark ecology" of Levinasian metaphysics. It engages recent attempts to extend Levinas's concept of "the face" (*le visage*) into the environmental sphere precisely by resisting such attempts. Levinas's ecology, instead, should be seen as providing us with a thorough account of the otherness of the environment and the strangeness of ecological life. Like the previous two chapters, this chapter recognizes the anonymity of the environment as one of the grand horrors of existence. Environmental ethics must begin from this premise if it is to make any progress confronting problems, like climate change, that exceed our capacity to conceptualize them.

Chapter 5 likewise takes up the quintessential Levinasian concept of the face. The face is often construed as a window on the transcendent that issues a divine ethical imperative and serves to institute an infinite responsibility for human suffering. This conception has undesirable social implications—the reinforcement of racial discrimination and colonialism, for instance—which are clarified by insights developed in critical race theory, feminist philosophy, and poststructuralism. The danger can be mitigated by treating the face as a material complexity which contains its own immanent imperative, a move that does not entail renouncing Levinas's notion of the face;

rather, it means attending to the face as a sensible infinity and tangible force. A mundane view of the face, grounded in its aesthetic singularity and material complexity, which follows the spirit but perhaps not the letter of Levinasian ethics, is adduced to illustrate this.

The book concludes with an essay on Alphonso Lingis as a unique heir to Levinas's theory of the subject. Lingis, exceptional among Levinas's interpreters, fully appreciates the materiality of Levinasian metaphysics and its aesthetic dimensions; he likewise has little patience for Levinasian piety. In a way, Lingis is the apostasy of Levinas. While Chapter 6 is not explicitly about Levinas, its purpose is to demonstrate what Levinas's texts are capable of producing when read against the grain.

As I draw this preface to a close it dawns on me that what links each of the chapters together—apart from the litany of themes already mentioned—is the sense of horror that looms over Levinas's ontology. This sense of horror is detectable in his mobilization of metaphors of darkness, shadow, insomnia, fatigue, strangeness, and the like, which double as proper metaphysical concepts in his texts. These concepts are, we could say, essential to any real encounter with the other *as other*. The other is by definition that which eludes us, escapes our attempts to catch hold of it both practically and intellectually. The other remains forever anonymous, unknown to us, and yet present to us. The dark presence of the other was never lost on Levinas. He recognized that there is something terrible and terrifying about existence, something that is perhaps summed up with a single word: *indifference*. This, I suspect, is why he insisted that we see ethics as first philosophy. Only a radical upheaval of our metaphysical priorities could confront indifference writ large, an indifference woven into the fabric of being and coursing through the veins of nature. But there is always the possibility that existence truly is nihilistic, which is to say, without ground and beyond our capacity to make sense of it. It is quite possible that

7

ethics is not first philosophy. In other words, it is possible that metaphysics describes a reality that is, in the final analysis, apathetically detached from our concerns and unmoved by the precariousness of our well-being. Levinas's deep appreciation of this horror is what I have tried to evoke in the following pages.

I am grateful to Cierra Clark, whose companionship gives me the energy to write and whose careful eyes helped prepare this text. A big thanks is also due to Dave Mesing for his diligent proofreading and friendship.

Tom Sparrow

Slippery Rock, Pennsylvania

Notes

1. Graham Harman, "Aesthetics as First Philosophy: Levinas and the Non-Human," *Naked Punch* 9 (2007): 21-30.

I

Darkest Hours

Introduction

Absent a comprehensive history of darkness and the night as philosophical metaphors, a history that would match the well-documented ubiquity of light as a metaphor, what I will say here about Levinas's deployment of the night could seem like little more than an ahistorical curiosity. But Levinas's analysis of the night is situated within at least three lines of thinking in the history of philosophy, each of which is tied to the Platonic legacy. And insofar as Levinas's discourse on the night contests this legacy's exultation of light and illumination—that is, contests the imagery which constitutes the very discourse of the Western philosophical tradition—we can regard his thinking as, in a certain sense, counter-philosophical.[1] The following remarks attempt to elucidate this counter-philosophical tendency and, in a modest way, contribute to what would be the conceptual history of the night. Levinas's 1947 text *Existence and Existents* provides the primary reference point.[2]

The three lines of thinking entered by Levinas's discourse on the night are: (1) the history of light as philosophical metaphor; (2) the history of ontology or metaphysics; and (3) the turn to the body in the twentieth century. It is with this latter trajectory that I am primarily concerned, and it is my interest in Levinas as both a philosopher of the body and a strange materialist that motivates my attention to his analysis of light, the night, and the insomniac's struggle with wakefulness. Indeed, it is via a critique of light in *Existence and Existents* that Levinas builds a metaphysical theory of the subject which, I contend, is basically materialist. This materialism is given explicit expression in the discourse on the night and it is concretized in the phenome-

9

nology of insomnia.

Metaphorics of Light

The metaphor of light plays a significant role in every period of philosophy's history, a role which is not reducible to an innocent literary trope. As Hans Blumenberg notes, "already in Plato…the *metaphorics* of light already has a *metaphysics* of light implicit in it."[3] The philosophical function of the light metaphor is evidenced by glancing at the work of Plato, Descartes, and Heidegger, each of whom informs Levinas's ethics in a fundamental way. In his descriptions of the transcendent goodness of the Other, Levinas draws on Plato's image of the sun as that which illuminates beings and thus enables vision and knowledge. The light which emanates from the sun, which in one sense represents the Good beyond being, figures as the divine source of what exists.[4] To quote Levinas: "Light, whether it emanates from the sensible or from the intelligible sun, is, since Plato, said to be the condition for all beings" (EE 40). In Descartes, from whom Levinas borrows the idea of infinity in order to characterize once again the transcendence of the Other, it is the natural light of reason, the *lumen naturale*, that intuits what is beyond our doubt and as such designated certain knowledge.[5] The natural light of reason, which is "[withdrawn from] all my senses" and all "images of corporeal things," is essential to rational self-reflection and the discovery of the *ego cogito*.[6] Finally, the image of light figures into Heidegger's notion of truth. Dasein serves as the *Lichtung*, or "lighted clearing," wherein being is disclosed or uncovered.[7] Levinas's critique of light seizes upon this notion of disclosure and its ubiquity in philosophical and phenomenological rhetoric.

On Levinas's account the "essential event" of the world is "intention and light" (EE 28-29). This is as the phenomenologist sees it. By "the world," Levinas here means Heidegger's world where beings are first and foremost an array of equipment to be grasped, manipulated, and employed as tools toward deter-minate human ends: "A being is what is thought about, seen, acted on, willed, felt—an object. Consequently, existence in the world always has a center; it is never anonymous" (EE 29). As he writes this, Levinas is preparing a decisive criticism of the luminosity of the subject-object correlation endemic to phenom-enology (and Heideggerian ontology), which in a sense includes Plato and Kant. Remarking on how the sun's rays bind together seer and seen, and thus constitute vision, Plato holds that "when the eyes are no longer turned upon objects upon whose colors the light of day falls but that of the dim luminaries of night, their edge is blunted and they appear almost blind..."[8] The problem with this perspective is that it restricts the realm of sense to what appears and has form; it disallows for meanings or significations that resist the ordering gaze of the ego. "What does not enter into the forms is banished from the world," Levinas says (EE 31).[9] This is because, for intentional consciousness, "sense is that by which what is exterior is already adjusted to and refers to what is interior" (EE 40). Its "light is that through which something is other than myself, but already as if it came from me."[10]

Ontology of the Night

The luminous view of the world entails, for Levinas, a reduction of the otherness of the given as well as a reduction of the challenge to theoretical consciousness that alterity poses: it assumes that everything that exists is graspable by the intellect and able to be encompassed by a totalizing vision. But it fails to notice that the intellect only grasps that which has "objective" sense, that is, has a form imposed on it: "Form is that by which a being is turned toward the sun, that by which it has a face, through which it gives itself, by which it comes forward" (EE 31). Consequently, and as Derrida will point out in "Violence and Metaphysics," by maintaining a primacy of intentionality and the subject-object correlation, the phenomenological conception of sense maintains an implicit violence which manifests in its reduction of the Other. In the phenomenological and ontological traditions, Derrida argues,

> there is a soliloquy of reason and a solitude of light. Incapable of respecting the Being and meaning of the other, phenomenology and ontology would be philosophies of violence. Through them, the entire philosophical tradition, in its meaning and at bottom, would make common cause with oppression and with the totalitarianism of the same. The ancient clandestine friendship between light and power, the ancient complicity between theoretical objectivity and technico-political possession.[11]

Whether the stakes are as dire as this passage suggests (and Levinas seems to see them as such), the seriousness of its portrayal fuels the urgency of Levinas's ethical project. His ethics necessitates a renunciation of light and a defense of those meanings which exceed the limits of theoretical apprehension. One such meaning is expressed in and by the body. Levinas's analysis of the night develops the ontological significance of the body's expressivity; the analysis of insomnia gives it a concrete, i.e. phenomenological, presentation. Against the primacy of the personal and theoretical, the night harbors a dark realm of sensuous materiality that is not without meaning, however negatively it must be conceived. As Cathryn Vasseleu puts it, "Night reveals the limits of phenomenology in the body's carnality."[12] Levinas's turn to the night serves as a reminder that to live is not simply to be conscious, but to find oneself caught in the grip of an alterity that not only approaches from the outside, but which wells up inside of us to disrupt and menace the smooth operation of the intellect and the cultivation of a solipsistic identity.

For Levinas any philosophy that privileges the form of beings over their materiality risks forcibly concealing the "nudity in which an undressed being withdraws from the world, and *is* as though its existence were elsewhere" (EE 31).[13] As we know, nearly the whole of Western philosophy is guilty of this kind of violence against alterity, whereas it is in Levinas's metaphysics that the nudity of beings—and especially the nudity of the human being—is most respected in its vulnerability. (Derrida, it should be noted, will show that Levinas could have done better.) The "relationship with nudity," Levinas maintains, "is the true experience of the otherness of the other" (EE 31). A philosophy of the night recognizes that form disintegrates in the darkness, objects lose their graspabilty, and the naked materiality of existence encroaches upon the meaning that light reveals. This must not be seen as simply a deficient mode of knowing, however, but as an intimate engagement with a carnal alterity. "Scandal takes cover in the night," says Levinas (EE 31), and it is in the night that the caress, voluptuousness, and desire find refuge. It is arguably under the cover of darkness that goodness, as fecundity,[14] is most productive. Each of these Levinasian catchwords (desire, fecundity, voluptuousness, caress) describes a certain encounter with the other as other, as that "objectless dimension" (EE 35) of nocturnal existence which humbles our will to consume or annihilate it:[15]

> In the random agitation of caresses there is the admission that access is impossible, violence fails, possession is refused. There is also the ridiculous and tragic simulation of devouring in kissing and love-bites. It is as though one had made a mistake about the nature of one's desire and had confused it with hunger which aims at something, but which one later found out was a hunger for nothing. (EE 35)

The night, Alphonso Lingis explains in what is assuredly a gloss on Levinas, is "not a substance, but an event." This event effaces identity, depersonalizes without destroying us.[16] Blanchot illustrates the point in *Thomas the Obscure* (1941):

The darkness immersed everything; there was no hope of passing through its shadows, but one penetrated its reality in a relationship of overwhelming intimacy. [Thomas's] first observation was that he could still use his body, and particularly his eyes; it was not that he saw anything, but what he looked at eventually placed him in contact with a nocturnal mass which he vaguely perceived to be himself and in which he was bathed.[17]

What, then, is produced by the "nocturnal" event that *Totality and Infinity* will designate as exceeding the "play of lights" which defines representational thinking and the adequation between consciousness and being?[18] A certain affective encounter with being qua being is produced, and thereby Levinasian ontology seeks to darken the metaphysics of light.

Levinas draws an ontological distinction within the night itself. Levinas differentiates between the night of the *il y a* (the "there is," or bare anonymous existence, which Levinas calls the "central concept" of *Existence and Existents* [EE 44]) and the phenomenal night which opposes daylight. In Heidegger's language, there is both an ontological and ontic understanding of the night. Vasseleu maintains that the former is synonymous with alterity and the trace of the Other, which is why she designates it as the "non-visual, non-ontological precursor of presence."[19] The *il y a*, she says, is unrelated to light, purely affective, and the source of a horror greater than the anxiety found in Heidegger's fundamental ontology.[20] Now, it may be the case that the *il y a* is prior to the hypostasis of an existent who actively takes up a position in being, but I would contend that the passivity suffered by the existent in the face of the *il y a*—that is, in the night—is itself an *ontological* event that reveals the basically heterological nature of embodied subjectivity.[21] In other words, ontology is not exhausted by the visible or the illuminable. Ontology suffers from a fundamental obscurity, opacity, and darkness.

It is also unnecessary to posit the *il y a* as beyond being or outside of immanence (immanence understood in the Spinozist or Deleuzean sense).[22] It is possible to think the separation of an existent as immanent to the rumble of the *il y a*, bare existence. This separation, however, need not be cast as a transcendence of being. This is what it would mean to think the advent of the subject as an event of being in its fundamental materiality or "elemental" nature (EE 44), rather than as an incarnation of a disembodied spirit. Indeed, to conceive the hypostasis, separation, or positioning of the subject as an effect of effort and labor and fatigue, as Levinas does in both *Existence and Existents* and *Totality and Infinity*, is to conceive subjectivity as the practical *production* (rather than reception) of form—clothing, dwellings, societal roles, etc., whatever cloaks bare existence in singular material effects and individuates the subject (EE 31).[23] Quoting *Existence and Existents* again,

> here materiality is thickness, coarseness, massivity, wretchedness. It is what has consistency, weight, is absurd, is a brute but impassive presence; it is also what is humble, bare and ugly. A material object, in being destined for a use, in forming part of a setting, is thereby clothed with a form which conceals its nakedness. The discovery of the *materiality of being* is not a discovery of a new quality, but of its *formless proliferation*. Behind the luminosity of forms, by which beings already relate to our 'inside', *matter is the very fact of the* there is... (EE 51, italics added)

Insofar as the materiality of the existent, the existent's body, is in touch with the *il y a*, Vasseleu is right to point out that the body for Levinas is the adventitious materialization of consciousness and that "consciousness begins as a sense of corporeality."[24] That is, separation begins in the formless rumblings of immanence. And the carnality of our sensibility is precisely what gets back in touch with the *il y a* when our bodies and minds dissolve into the night. It would not be accurate to describe this as an "experience" of the *il y a*, Levinas insists (EE 52), because the term "experience" is "inapplicable to a situation which involves the total exclusion of light." The night is non-discursive, an immediate encounter with a pure nothingness (or a pure plenitude?) that is nevertheless an impersonal *something*: "What we call the I is itself submerged by the night, invaded, depersonalized, stifled by it. The disappearance of all things and of the I leaves what cannot appear, the sheer fact of being in which *one* participates, whether one wants to or not, without having taken the initiative, anonymously" (EE 53). The night opens us up to a signification that can only be apprehended by the body, the body taken not as a prosthesis of a situated, perspectival consciousness (as in Merleau-Ponty, who will not allow the night to completely destroy personal identity[25]), but rather as an event that is without perspective and lacking intentional directedness (EE 53).

The body engulfed in nocturnal space has no point of reference; it is a sentience reduced to its affectivity or sensibility, which *Totality and Infinity* calls enjoyment[26] and *Existence and Existents* denotes as horror (EE 54-55). Material life is a frightening joy. The horror of the night presents us with an "indeterminate menace" in which "one is exposed" to the "dark background of existence" (EE 55), that is, to the materiality and mortality of being—in other words, to all the forces which restrict our freedom as embodied, *contingent* beings who nonetheless remain *necessarily* riveted to their being. The contradiction of this position is perhaps what makes it so unsettling or tragic. "Horror carries out the condemnation to perpetual reality, to existence with 'no exits'" (EE 58).[27] Maybe it is this "insecurity" in the face of existence that Elie Wiesel had in mind when he gave the title

Night to his recollection of the Holocaust.[28] Wiesel illustrates Levinas's point that daylight is not exempt from the horror of the night when he writes: "We received no food. We lived on snow; it took the place of bread. The days resembled the nights, and the nights left in our souls the dregs of their darkness. The train rolled slowly, often halted for a few hours, and continued. It never stopped snowing. We remained lying on the floor for days and nights, one on top of the other, never uttering a word. We were nothing but frozen bodies. Our eyes closed, we merely waited for the next stop, to unload our dead."

Tangible Darkness

The night is not just a metaphysical concept for Levinas; it has a concrete modality. It is the insomniac who experiences the night phenomenologically, but she is also the one who succumbs to the horrifying absence of form featured in insomnia. The insomniac wills herself to sleep, to take leave of the night, but instead the anonymous "field of forces" that constitute existence disallows her rest and commands her vigilance.[29] She is kept awake by something. Insomnia catches the subject up in its immanence, terrorizes consciousness (EE 62) and seizes the body, revealing the shadowy depths of the gift of being. It is the realization that being's truth is not always exhibited in the light of day, but is sometimes—even essentially—delivered under the cloak of darkness and in the deafening silence of insomnia, that marks Levinas's deployment of the night.

In the last analysis, Levinas does not make the anonymity of the night the transcendental condition of separation, or hypostasis. As he says, "It is necessary to bring out this experience of depersonalization *before compromising it* through a reflection on its conditions" (EE 63, italics added). Although the *il y a* is experienced in insomnia, an encounter with bare existence, being reduced to nothingness, is accessible (perhaps) only through a thought experiment (cf. EE 51-52). The ontology of the night cannot be circumscribed by phenomenology. Are we to infer from this that existence is never actually anonymous? And if we never directly, but only imaginatively, experience the pure "rustling" of the *il y a* (EE 61), what permits us to affirm its independent reality? Should we not remind Levinas that darkness does not actually dissolve all forms, that each of the non-visual senses has its own means of apprehending the contours of objects? Also, we must ask again, with Derrida,[30] whether the privilege granted to the face of the Other, whose "epiphany" institutes the ethical command, can escape the violence of light which Levinas works so hard to undo. Or perhaps the displacement of philosophy effected by Levinas's discourse on the night, and its attendant ontology, are sufficient to recast the light with a nonviolent meaning and to assign being an essentially oppressive role. It depends, I think, on whether the *il y a* is, ontologically speaking, *first* either a menace to the already separated existent or the divine source of its separation. This uncertain disjunction haunts Levinas's texts.

Notes

1. Recognizing the hegemony of light in the history of philosophy and the metaphorics of light in language as such, Derrida contends rightly that "it is difficult to maintain a philosophical discourse against light." Jacques Derrida, "Violence and Metaphysics: An Essay on the Thought of Emmanuel Levinas," in *Writing and Difference*, trans. Alan Bass (Chicago: University of Chicago Press, 1978), 85, 92.

2. Emmanuel Levinas, *Existence and Existents*, trans. Alphonso Lingis (Pittsburgh: Duquesne University Press, 1988). Hereafter cited in the text as EE.

3. See Hans Blumenberg's "Light as a Metaphor for Truth," in *Modernity and the Hegemony of Vision*, ed. David Michael Levin (Berkeley: University of California Press, 1993).

4. Plato, *Republic*, trans. Paul Shorey, in *The Collected Dialogues*

of Plato, eds. Edith Hamilton and Huntington Cairns (Princeton: Princeton University Press, 1989), 508a-509a. For example, see Levinas, *Otherwise than Being; or, Beyond Essence*, trans. Alphonso Lingis (Pittsburgh: Duquesne University Press, 1991), 19. Note that when I use "Other" (capitalized) I mean the human other exclusively.

5. René Descartes, *Meditations on First Philosophy*, in *Philosophical Essays and Correspondence*, ed. Roger Ariew (Indianapolis: Hackett, 2000), 115. Blumenberg, "Light as a Metaphor for Truth" (35), indicates that "natural light" (*lumen naturale*) is an expression coined by Cicero.

6. Descartes, *Meditations*, 113.

7. Martin Heidegger, *Being and Time*, trans. John Macquarrie and Edward Robinson (New York: HarperCollins, 1962), §28.

8. Plato, *Republic*, 508c.

9. Levinas puts the point pithily in "Phenomenon and Enigma," in *Collected Philosophical Papers*, trans. Alphonso Lingis (Pittsburgh: Duquesne University Press, 1987), 70: "Phenomena, apparition in the full light, the relationship with being, ensure immanence as a totality and philosophy as atheism. The enigma, the intervention of a meaning which disturbs phenomena but is quite ready to withdraw like an undesirable stranger, unless one harkens to those footsteps that depart, is transcendence itself, the proximity of the other as other."

10. Emmanuel Levinas, *Time and the Other*, trans. Richard A. Cohen (Pittsburgh: Duquesne University Press, 1987), 64.

11. Derrida, "Violence and Metaphysics," 91.

12. Cathryn Vasseleu, *Textures of Light: Vision and Touch in Irigaray, Levinas and Merleau-Ponty* (London: Routledge, 1998), 86.

13. It seems as though Levinas (citing Aristotle) sees form as a finite limitation imposed on matter, which is infinite. Intentionality is responsible for this imposition; it makes

things graspable as objects (EE 33). Consider his remark (EE 47) that, "A word cannot be separated from meaning. But there is first the materiality of the sound...." On Levinas's concern with materiality in *Otherwise than Being*, see John Drabinski, *Sensibility and Singularity: The Problem of Phenomenology in Levinas* (Albany: SUNY Press, 2001), 167-219.

14. On fecundity as the production of goodness, alterity, and as paternity, see Levinas, *Totality and Infinity: An Essay on Exteriority*, trans. Alphonso Lingis (Pittsburgh: Duquesne University Press, 1969), 267-269.

15. This point is made in Levinas's discussion of the impossibility of murder and the impotence of the murderous act. See, for instance, "Philosophy and the Idea of Infinity," in *Collected Philosophical Papers*, 55.

16. Alphonso Lingis, *The Imperative* (Bloomington: Indiana University Press, 1994), 9, 10.

17. Maurice Blanchot, *Thomas the Obscure*, in *The Station Hill Blanchot Reader*, ed. George Quasha (Barrytown, NY: Station Hill, 1999), 60.

18. In *Totality and Infinity*, 27-28, Levinas tells us that conscious events are not primarily disclosures, but rather *productions*. These events, moreover, he characterizes as "nocturnal."

19. Vasseleu, *Textures of Light*, 85.

20. *Textures of Light*, 83-84.

21. Levinas distinguishes in *Time and the Other* (64) between the separation accorded to the ego by light/reason and the "ontological event of the subject's materiality."

22. Levinas is on the surface allergic to immanentist ontology because of the threat it poses to freedom and ipseity, as when he dismissively declares in *Totality and Infinity* that "Spinoza conjures away separation" (119). I think a sufficiently complex immanent ontology can satisfy Levinas's concern for the Other, even if this ontology could not possibly follow

the *spirit* of Levinas's text, but only its letter. I am thinking here of Levinas's image of the "coiling" self in *Totality and Infinity* (118) and the image of involution or enfolding it elicits; see also his remarks on the self as folding back (*repli*) on itself in EE 81.

23. See "The Dwelling" in Levinas, *Totality and Infinity*.

24. Vasseleu, *Textures of Light*, 87.

25. The night, in Merleau-Ponty, *Phenomenology of Perception*, trans. Colin Smith (London: Routledge, 1962), 283, "is not an object" and "has no outlines." "[I]t enwraps me and infiltrates through all my senses, stifling my recollections and almost destroying my personal identity." I see Merleau-Ponty's refusal to allow the night to totally depersonalize as a consequence of his privileging of perception—which is at bottom personal—over the anonymity of sensation, which Levinas allows for. Merleau-Ponty does acknowledge the ability of the night to remind us of our contingency, however, which is something that Levinas does not make explicit in his discussion.

26. Levinas, *Totality and Infinity*, 135-137.

27. On the freedom afforded us by consciousness and the separation of the ego from being, see EE 37, 38, 42-43.

28. Elie Wiesel, *Night*, trans. Marion Wiesel (New York: Hill and Wang, 2006), 100. It is perhaps what Levinas calls the "vigilance" of the insomniac—a wakefulness without object—that allowed Wiesel to endure the horror of the Holocaust.

29. See Levinas, *Time and the Other*, 48.

30. Derrida, "Violence and Metaphysics," 92.

2

The Spectator's Shadow

Introduction

In what follows I give a reading of Levinas's aesthetics that draws out his non-phenomenological tendencies because, at the end of the day, I think the most fascinating aspects of Levinas's philosophy are those that exceed his commitment to phenomenology and bring him closer to someone like Deleuze, who is often regarded as antithetical to Levinas in particular, and phenomenology in general. Motivating my reading is the fact that both Levinas and Deleuze assign a transcendental function to sensation, which is interesting because it points to a kind of partnership between the two as philosophers of immanence. However, the main purpose of this chapter is not to build bridges. I am, I suspect, even more motivated by a remark I once received from an anonymous reviewer who was *disturbed* upon learning that I do indeed believe Levinas and Deleuze have much in common, ontologically speaking. Here's what the reader said: "I am not sure how to understand the transition from Levinas, who is so concerned with ethics, to Deleuze, whose commitment to [a] kind of ontological flattening...would exactly preclude a serious conception of ethics." Now, either this reader was unwilling to concede that a legitimate plurality of readings of Levinas is possible, or they were incapable of imagining that a Deleuzean ethics is possible. Incidentally, a book published in 2011, called *Deleuze and Ethics*, testifies to the actuality of a Deleuzean ethics, and therefore the possibility of a promising confrontation with Levinas.[1] To accomplish my reading, I should note, it is not necessary to establish that Deleuze is a closet Levinasian, which I do not think is right. Instead, I think it is more advantageous to show that Levinas is closer to Deleuze than Levinasians like to admit. To establish this, a different approach to Levinas is needed, one that reads him as a philosopher concerned *primarily* with the materiality of existence.

I want to make some sense of how the concepts of diachrony, representation, and sensation are mobilized in the aesthetics of Levinas. To accomplish this, I bring Levinas into dialogue with two unlikely allies: Gilles Deleuze and, to a much lesser degree, Jacques Rancière. My claim is that Levinas's critique of representation is arguably the most radical of those found in the phenomenological tradition, and in this respect he is philosophically very close to the Deleuze we find in *Francis Bacon: The Logic of Sensation*. What both thinkers share is a remarkable appreciation of the function of sensation, which is for both, I suggest, the basic element of aesthetics and the most fundamental element of experience. Sensation, however, is a problematic concept for the phenomenologist to incorporate into his analyses of experience because the logic of sensation identified by Levinas is not something disclosed phenomenologically. It is, as Deleuze says, invisible. Levinas better than any other phenomenologist achieves an integration of sensation into his philosophy, but this comes at the price of compromising the methodological integrity of his phenomenology and leaving us with the question of sensation's metaphysical status. This compromise is what draws him close to Deleuze, and it is also what enables us to ask about the emancipatory potential of Levinasian aesthetics. The question of emancipation, which I will only hint at here, is well-framed by the work of Rancière, whose writings on the image and the spectator provide a useful context for interrogating the political dimension of Levinas's aesthetics.

The Invasion of Shadow

One day not too long ago I was re-reading Levinas's 1948 essay "Reality and Its Shadow" and trying to focus explicitly on what reality means for Levinas, what reality's shadow is, and whether or not art possesses a special ability to disclose the real. Motivating my focus was a curiosity about whether or not Levinas could be considered a metaphysical realist, and if this hypothetical realism was compatible with phenomenology. This, along with some striking remarks he makes about sensation, led me to ask a few questions: *What function does sensation play in Levinas's view of spectatorship? Is Levinas's spectator merely subjected to the work of art, just the passive recipient of aesthetic experience, or is aesthetic experience more akin to the dialogical sense-experience Merleau-Ponty envisions when he's writing about Cézanne?* While reading Levinas, however, I found myself always thinking not about Merleau-Ponty, but about Deleuze.[2] Levinas consistently talks about sensation and aesthetic experience in terms that conceive the spectator as a kind of hostage to sensation, and this is precisely what brought Deleuze to my mind. Deleuze is, after all, one of the most vocal advocates of sensation in twentieth-century philosophy. Levinas writes this in "Reality and Its Shadow": "[The experience of aesthetic rhythm] represents a unique situation where we cannot speak of consent, assumption, initiative or freedom, because the subject is caught up and carried away by it. The subject is part of its own representation."[3] In other texts, he uses the same language to describe our encounter with the Other; he uses this language to describe our relation to existence in early works like *Existence and Existents* (1947), which is contemporary with "Reality and Its Shadow." And he continues to use this language in some important essays from the 1980s, which I discuss below. To be sure, a concern with the subject's participatory role in its representations spans the breadth of Levinas's work. What could it mean to say "that subject is part of its own representation?"

Not unlike Deleuze's interpretation of the painting of Francis Bacon, Levinas understands aesthetic experience in general, not just music or poetry or dance, as the locus of *rhythm*. It is the rhythm of the work of art that exerts a force on the spectator; or, rather, what *forces* the spectator to participate in the work of art. Understanding the nature of this force and this participation is essential to conceptualizing Levinas's aesthetics.

To say that the subject is part of its representation is not to make the Hegelian point that reason is constitutive of reality,[4] or that the subject actively shapes its reality through its conceptual and perceptual grasp of the world around it; or, as Levinas would put it, that to conceptualize the other is always to reduce the other to the same. To say that the subject is part of its representation is also not to echo Guy Debord's criticism, famously proclaimed in *The Society of the Spectacle*, that contemporary capitalist society presents us with nothing more than an image-mediated social relationship beyond which there is nothing real to see. "Far from welcoming any human activity that would challenge its authority," writes Debord, the "attitude that [the spectacular society] demands in principle is the same passive acceptance that it has already secured by means of its seeming incontrovertibility, and indeed by its monopolization of the realm of appearances."[5] Indeed, Levinas's point is quite the opposite of both the idealist and the Situationist. The spectacle of reality is, first and foremost, not a product of mediation. For Levinas, it is an immediacy: our representation of reality—*insofar as this representation is sensible*—takes hold of the subject who represents, and not necessarily in any superficial or exploitative mode. (Those modes are possible, of course, and Deleuze will even attach to these modes a particular kind of violence.) The forced participation induced by the spectacle on the spectator is, in Levinas's view, a means by which the real communicates with the spectator. The revelation of the real, however, does not occur in the represented or figurative content of the spectacle; it occurs *in the body*. The body is the locus of revelation, but not simply as something *to which* the spectacle is revealed. The body does not merely reflect what is contained in the spectacle, it *becomes* part of the spectacle itself. This is why reality cannot be said to reside outside of the image, the performance, the spectacle, or the represented; each of these domains contains a sensible dimension that affects the body to some degree, however minimal or redundant.

The move from acting in the world, either intellectually or practically, to beholding the world in the work of art[6] would seem to entail a movement from the position of active agent to passive recipient. When I seek to use an object, I reach out and take hold of it and mobilize it as a piece of equipment meant to fulfill my desires, my projects, or my whims. The object's alterity is destined to become synchronized with my *teloi*, locked into the ends I seek to actualize and rendered graspable in its presence. Intentionality, both practical or thematic, lies behind all of these acts of seizure, which is why Levinas writes in "Diachrony and Representation" (1985):

> Seeing or knowing, and taking in hand, are linked in the structure of intentionality, which remains the intrigue of a kind of thought that recognizes itself in consciousness: the "at-handness" [*main-tenance*] of the present emphasizes its immanence as the characteristic virtue of this sort of thought.[7]

When I seek to know an object, I set my mind the task of rendering that object intelligible by converting it into concepts that capture its essential characteristics and modalities. To know or to use an object is to take interest in it in one way or another, and to distill its being for an ego that would see, know, or use it.[8] Concepts and categories make the other manageable for the ego; the body schema makes the other useable for the embodied agent. Art, however, is meant to suspend this interestedness. It compels us, either by choice or by compulsion, to interrupt our grasp of the world in favor of the free play of our imagination. Or, at least, it offers a means of satisfying our curiosity. Whatever the case may be, aesthetic contemplation entails a disruption of our intentional life: "An image marks a hold over us rather than our initiative, a fundamental passivity."[9] This is the effect of what Levinas calls a work's rhythm. The detour of the practical and thematic modes of intentionality introduced by rhythm, which occurs in aesthetic experience of every type, introduces a measure of diachrony into the representational life of the ego.

Diachrony—which he describes in temporal terms as a "delay" and in visual terms as a "shadow"[10]—emerges immanently within consciousness, but as nonintentional; it does not come from outside and it does not point to a reality exclusive to artistic representation. It points to a reality that resonates in the body. Or rather, the body lives a time that is out of step with the ego. It signals a reality that belongs to the sensible dimension of any spectacle, and which Levinas can only describe as a kind of magical evasion of presence.[11]

In its simple modality, art substitutes an image of the object for the actual object. The object's presence is substituted by the presence of an image that re-presents the object in its absence. Hyperrealism would, at the limit, entail a kind of synchronization of these presences. None of this, however, fully describes what *happens* when I behold an image. Levinas, we already know, settles on the concept of rhythm to depict the effect of the image on the spectator. Images possess a fundamental musicality that Levinas finds embedded in their qualities. All the action occurs in the qualities. Or rather, it is an object's multiplicity of qualities (artistic or not) that gives it rhythm and makes it something *more* and something *other* than a unified substance, something dynamic. And it is at the level of our sensibility, that is, below the level of our apperception and the gathering of intentionality, that we are forced to participate in the rhythm of images. "The idea of rhythm," writes Levinas,

designates not so much an inner law of poetic order as the way the poetic order affects us, closed wholes whose elements

27

call for one another like the syllables of a verse, but do so only insofar as they impose themselves on us, disengaging themselves from reality. *But they impose themselves on us without our assuming them.* Or rather, our consenting to them is inverted into a participation. Their entry into us is one with our entry into them.[12]

Distinctive about this forced participation in the rhythm of the image—which is analogous, by Levinas's own admission, to the way one gets carried away by a song to the point of dancing involuntarily to it—is that it entails a loss of one's identity, "a passage of oneself to anonymity." Aesthetic existence involves a dislocation of oneself into the shadow of reality, an unhinging of the capacity to see, know, and do. For Levinas, it is not so much that sensation is disorganized, but that sensation is ungraspable. Sensation is what enables grasping, both conceptual and practical. It is what gives birth to concepts and practices, which always lag behind the imperatives of sensation.

The ontological dimension of sensation is not necessarily proper to art, even though it is often easiest to speak about aesthetic rhythm in the context of art. Art, however, enables us to catch sight of a mode of experience that necessarily unfolds between the conscious and the unconscious. It evinces a liminal experience that lies somewhere between the potential and the actual, the latent and the explicit, the transparent and the obscure. This is why Levinas describes art as "the very event of obscuring, a descent of the night, an invasion of shadow."[13] To be caught up in the rhythm of an artistic product—an image, song, dance, or poem—is to be deprived of freedom at the very same moment that one is involved in playing along with the work of art. To be caught up in rhythm is to present these opposing tendencies, the passive and the active, simultaneously in one's body. Levinas explains in the following terms: "The particular automatic character of a walk or a dance to music is a mode of being where nothing is unconscious, but where consciousness, paralyzed in its freedom, plays, totally absorbed in this playing."[14] By the same token, to be the spectator of an image is not to take in the image distinterestedly in the sense of finding no interest in it. On the contrary, to behold an image is to take interest in it as something intriguing and something to be taken into, *involved* with (in the strict sense) as participant.

Involvement in the spectacle is not equivalent to Heidegger's being-in-the-world, where one finds oneself among things to be mastered or gawked at or mulled over. Nor is it a separation from the spectacle, a merely observational involvement. Aesthetic involvement is participation in what Levinas calls the "pathos of the imaginary world of dreams," where the spectator finds herself pulled into the spectacle and out of herself—out of the *here* that constitutes her historical being-there, the ground of her freedom, what Heidegger calls her Dasein and what Levinas calls her position.[15] Aesthetic experience is the rendering exterior of one's interiority, a sacrifice of one's agency to the invisible rhythm of the material world.[16] The exteriorization of oneself in the work of art is not analogous to the time-consciousness of Husserl or the ecstatic temporalization of Dasein elaborated by Heidegger, both of which entail a recuperation or retrieval of oneself.[17] The exteriorization of the spectator in the spectacle is induced by the diachrony of the spectacle, which involves the spectator in an impersonal, elemental past that Levinas sometimes refers to as the transcendental function of sensation, or what we might call the temporality of sensation. Levinas identifies this in numerous texts—often in reference to the other, God, or the infinite—as a past which has never been present.

Aesthetic experience is numbered among the forms of nonintentional consciousness because it involves the subject as a locus of *affectivity* rather than reflection, intelligibility, or directedness.[18] The affective does not belong either to the extensive or the intentional; it belongs instead to the *intensive* dimension of reality, which is incapable of reflecting a representation or figuration. As affective, spectatorship is, in Levinas's phrase, the very "ruin of representation." Instead of a kind of fulfillment or satisfaction of desire, it is a form of suffering. We see that this kind of suffering, however, signals nothing other than the emancipatory potential of the aesthetic. This means that art, for instance, has the ability to affect us with an intensity that bypasses the intentional or conceptual in order to take hold directly of the senses. This is possible because both the work of art as spectacle and the body of the spectator belong to the matter of the world and trade in the very same qualities that compose the rhythm of matter. As affective, the rhythm of the work of art has the capacity—and in some instances, explicitly aims—to plunge the spectator into the darkness of being, into a nocturnal anarchy of the senses which Levinas dramatizes in *Existence and Existents*. Just as the night stages a confrontation with an exteriority that provides no correlation with interiority, leaving the subject with no perspective from which to grasp its surroundings, art is "a descent of the night"[19] that has the power to render the I "submerged [...], invaded, depersonalized, stifled by it. The disappearance of all things and of the I leaves what cannot disappear, the sheer fact of being in which *one* participates, whether one wants to or not, without having taken the initiative, anonymously."[20] Even though Levinas is talking here about the impersonality and indifference of being, what he ultimately is speaking about is the anonymous materiality of sensation, not as the matter of perception, but as the infinite, ungraspable yet tangible element of aesthetic events.[21] While this may sound terrifying, it is nevertheless a necessary condition of aesthetic edification. To learn from the work of art is to suffer its lesson, to have oneself transformed by what it teaches.

The sensory qualities, or elements, of art are unlike the sensory qualities of an object insofar as the latter indicate a substantial unity to which the qualities point, beyond their multiplicity. In Husserl's language, beyond the series of adumbrations that I perceive lies the noematic core of the object. In other words, these adumbrations are the stepping stones that get us to the object in its objective presence. In art we find that sensations are not a mere means that refer us beyond themselves: they *are* the object sought by the spectator. Sensations constitute the aesthetic event's materiality, the reality that makes up the rhythm or musicality of the work of art.[22] To look beyond art's surface qualities is, in a sense, to misapprehend the work of art as rhythm or musicality:

> To insist on the musicality of every image is to see in an image its detachment from an object, that independence from the category of substance which the analysis of our textbooks ascribe to pure sensation not yet converted into perception (sensation as an adjective), which for empirical psychology remains a limit case, a purely hypothetical given.[23]

It is within images that we get sensation itself. It is there encountered as something more than a pure posit of cognition or an inferred residue of perception. In images sensation operates with a function all its own: i.e. to convert the spectator—via its rhythm—into a participant in the spectacle itself. But lest we conclude that this is a function proper to art, Levinas insists that insofar as any part of the world can become an image,[24] the whole of the world has the power to seize us with its rhythm. Sensation operates within an "ontological dimension that does not extend between us and a reality to be captured;" it marks the immanence of a reality we participate in anonymously and nonintentionally.[25]

Art is thus a doubling of reality. But not insofar as it stands in for a "real" world beyond its surface, but insofar as it is a presence that resembles and dissembles itself simultaneously.

The Force of Sensation

This way of thinking about the immanence of sensation, the aesthetic event, and the exteriority involved in spectatorship is much closer to Deleuze than it is to Husserl, Heidegger, or even Merleau-Ponty. And indeed, it is this nonphenomenological dimension of Levinas's philosophy that I find so fascinating. As he writes in "Reality and Its Shadow": "The phenomenology of images insists on their transparency. The intention of one who contemplates an image is said to go directly through the image, as through a window, into the world it represents, and aims at an *object*."[26] Phenomenology in this respect fails to take the image on its own terms, as an object bearing its own reality. Its emphasis on the significance of representation is what turns Levinas away from the phenomenology of art. There is a distinct move away from the figurative and signification in Levinas's analyses; he cares less about what images point to or intend, and much more about how a representation's qualities open up a fissure in its being and time. Deleuze will describe this as the *"shallow depth…that rips the painting away from all narrative as well as from all symbolization."*[27] Even when it attends to the qualitative dimension, phenomenology, Levinas insists, privileges the synchronization of thought and world, otherwise called "presence," as well as the theoretical, discursive, and knowable. Even if there is in Merleau-Ponty a move away from this privileging, and a turn toward the corporeal dimension of lived experience, the correlation of thought and being in phenomenology is never really contested by the diachrony introduced into representation by sensation.[28]

Readers of Deleuze will recognize the line of thought that I have traced in Levinas's work. As Deleuze interprets him, what interests Francis Bacon is the way in which the "invisible forces" of sensation mold, sculpt, "model," or "shake" the flesh of the spectator.[29] These forces are transmitted precisely through the rhythm of painting, which forms its very essence.[30] Rhythm, likewise, is what animates sensation, according to Deleuze. This is why he should be read alongside Levinas.

What does rhythm accomplish in Deleuze's aesthetics, and what does sensation have to do with rhythm? As Dan Smith explains, "Aesthetic comprehension is the grasping of a rhythm with regard to both the thing to be measured and the unit of measure."[31] This grasping, however, is not the violent grasping denounced by Levinas; this is because it is accomplished *without a concept*. It is instead, as Deleuze says, a submersion of oneself in the spectacle, an exploration of the rhythms that serve as the "ground" of aesthetic comprehension and the vitality of sensation. The phenomenology of perception, with its thesis of the primacy of perception, is invalidated precisely by this point. This vitality not only animates the spectacle as qualitative multiplicity, it likewise animates the spectator: "at one and the same time I *become* in the sensation and something *happens* through the sensation, one through the other, one in the other. And at the limit, it is the same body that, being both subject and object, gives and receives the sensation. As a spectator, I experience the sensation only be entering the painting, by reaching the unity of the sensing and the sensed."[32] Sensation, for Deleuze as for Levinas, works directly on the spectator and has the effect of forcing the spectator into the position of participant in the spectacle. Sensation does not need to be communicated through a sign, symbol, or concept. It is the body that comprehends, or rather accommodates, the power of sensation.[33]

For Deleuze, as we have seen with Levinas, sensations are not strictly identical to qualities; such an equivalence would threaten to reduce sensations to the level of mere appearance, epiphenomena, or subjective data. Sensations are more than this: they bear upon our bodies with an "intensive reality," and it is this reality that pulls the body outside itself, renders it ecstatic and other than itself. "Sensation is a vibration," a rhythm.[34] The way the body vibrates with sensations determines how, and to what

33

degree, it is molded and deformed by aesthetic events, and to what extent it "takes on an excessive and spasmodic appearance, exceeding the bounds of organic activity." This excess is what Bacon aims to paint in his screams.[35] "If we scream," writes Deleuze, "it is always as victims of invisible and insensible forces that scramble every spectacle, and that even lie beyond pain and feeling."[36] Here again the horror of sensation rears its head. The aim of painting is to make these forces visible, which is not to represent these forces as concepts or signifying traits. Painting is meant to *affect* the spectator, to exert a force on sensibility that disrupts the spectator's organic unity and which lies within the ruins of the spectacle's representational content, that is, in its unrepresentable and ungraspable rhythms. Against phenomenology, Deleuze writes: "the lived body is still a paltry thing in comparison with a more profound and almost unlivable Power [*Puissance*]." The unity of this power, or rhythm, can only be sought "at the point where rhythm itself plunges into chaos, into the night, at the point where the [different levels of sensation] are perpetually and violently mixed."[37] All of this, for Deleuze, requires a supplanting of the violence of the spectacle by the violence of sensation. What does this mean?

Pain and violence figure prominently in Deleuze's treatment of Bacon's painting and loom over Levinas's aesthetics. Violence and pain are linked, for both thinkers, to the inadequacy of both thought and body to undergo what art *does* to us. And what art does is always at least partly a question of the intensity of its sensations. For Levinas, the force of sensation entails a disintegration of one's perspective on the world that is analogous to the horror one experiences in the face of the "there is" (*il y a*), the bare fact of existence.[38] There is also a marked violence involved in the act of knowing or comprehending, which necessarily reduces the alterity of what is known. For Deleuze, the violence of the spectacle is twofold. There is a violence of the represented, such as we find in the paintings and prints of Goya.[39] There is also the violence of sensation, which, as we have seen, bypasses any narrative and impacts the nervous system directly.[40] This is violence taken as a violation of the body. To supplant the representational violence of the spectacle with the violence of sensation means, at least in one sense, to create art that forces the body to confront realities that operate on it at the affective level and compel it to express or perform these forces in its movements—movements that push it beyond itself, into something other than itself, without destroying it or getting it caught up in banal meanings and distractions. As Deleuze writes:

> When, like a wrestler, the visible body confronts the powers of the invisible, it gives them no other visibility than its own. It is within this visibility that the body actively struggles, affirming the possibility of triumphing, which was beyond its reach as long as these powers remained invisible, hidden in a spectacle that sapped our strength and diverted us.[41]

Levinas, too, entreats us to overcome the spectacle by wrestling with its hidden forces. But he also offers an alternative means of eliminating the spectacle. To behold an image, for instance, is to take it as a representation of an absent reality that it resembles. It substitutes one form of presence for another, both of which refer us to the same object. But the image is a reality in its own right, albeit one that is doubled. On the face of it, its figure or representative content tells a story or signifies something or other. This is merely a "caricature" of the image, one aspect of it. The rest of the image, its invisible forces, remain hidden from view even as they operate on our senses. A spectacle, then—whether an object, a work of art, or a performance—is "that which is, that which reveals itself in its truth, and, at the same time, it resembles itself, is its own image. The original gives itself as though it were at a distance from itself, as though it were withdrawing itself, as

35

though something in a being delayed behind being." The diachrony of representation, the doubling of the spectacle as idol or allegory of itself, is the very structure of the sensible: "The sensible is being insofar as it resembles itself, insofar as, outside of its triumphal work of being, it casts a shadow, emits that obscure and elusive essence, that phantom essence which cannot be identified with the essence revealed in truth."[42] Reality always resembles itself, while every representation always ends up proliferating the dimensions of the real. To see straight through to the object represented is to neglect the surprises that lurk in the shadows of reality.

Horrors of Emancipation

Levinas has, perhaps, much less in common with Rancière than he does with Deleuze. Nevertheless, I think it is worth noting a modest point of convergence because it helps us shed some light on the emancipatory potential of the suffering, violence, and horror of Levinas's aesthetics. In *The Emancipated Spectator* Rancière defines the spectator as one who is "separated from both the capacity to know and the power to act."[43] In Levinas's language, a spectator would be someone who confronts, yet lacks the ability to grasp the other and, therefore, fails to reduce the other to the same. The spectator is effectively what the insomniac is for Levinas, a subject incapable of escaping, either practically or mentally, the presence of the night.[44] For Levinas, the spectator's capacity to know or act upon the other is interrupted by the other's elusive qualities, their withdrawal from the caricature that our representations make of them.[45] In other words, it is because the spectator is caught up within the doubling of the spectacle that they lack the capacity to take hold of it in thought or deed.

For Rancière, the question of the spectator is the question of who polices the distance between artistic spectacles and their spectators. In other words, who determines the extent to which the spectator may participate in and comprehend the knowledge embedded in the spectacle? Rancière suggests that it may be the artist himself, despite his deliberate attempts to engage the spectator—to make him or her enter or enact the work of art—and draw out of him or her the knowledge required to comprehend the work of art. Rancière sees in Situationists like Debord, and Marxist theory more generally, a failure to eradicate the spectator's distance from the spectacle precisely because they (Marxists, Situationists) operate with a logic that deploys in its critique the very oppositions that must be abandoned.

The question of who actively creates art and who merely observes it trades upon a distinction between viewing and knowing that is not a purely logical opposition, but rather a product of a certain distribution of the sensible, what Rancière identifies as "an *a priori* distribution of the positions and capacities and incapacities attached to these positions."[46] Even in contemporary art, despite attempts to erode the distinction, the spectator is cast as a passive participant in the spectacle, whereas the one who stages the spectacle is charged with mastery of the spectacle's knowledge, its "point." Until this opposition is eroded or overcome, the spectator will never be capable of making their own sense of the work of art precisely because they will never be in the position—*as* spectator—of independent thinker. For Rancière, "emancipation begins when we challenge the opposition between viewing and acting; when we understand that the self-evident facts that structure the relations between saying, seeing and doing themselves belong to the structure of domination and subjection."[47]

As it does for Rancière, the emancipatory dimension of Levinas's aesthetics trades on the blurring of the oppositions we maintain between viewer and knower, active and passive, creator and consumer, etc. We have seen that at the aesthetic level sensation enacts an elision of the distinction between interior and exterior as well as active and passive. The concept of rhythm accomplishes an understanding of performance that places animation neither in the hands of the one who performs nor in the forces that carry the body along. The spectator is part of the spectacle, not separated from it. This is Levinas's logic of sensation.

For Rancière, to close the gap between spectator and spectacle, what is required is a logic of emancipation that works to undo the distribution of the sensible which cannot conceive the role of the spectator as anything other than a passive viewer. The logic of emancipation conceives the transmission of knowledge not as a one-way street, but as something that is discovered by everyone individually and on their own terms. This is possible because

> between the ignorant schoolmaster and the emancipated novice there is always a third thing—a book or some other piece of writing—alien to both and to which they can refer to verify in common what the pupil has seen, what she says about it and what she thinks of it. The same applies to performance. It is not the transmission of the artist's knowledge or inspiration to the spectator. It is the third thing that is owned by no one whose meaning is owned by no one, but which subsists between them, excluding any uniform transmission, any identity of cause and effect.[48]

What is central here is the idea that meaning is what resides between individuals as something accessible by everyone, and which is, strictly speaking, common and anonymous. It belongs to no one and is accessible to anyone willing to witness, engage, and articulate the spectacle in their own way. The power of the spectator, in Rancière's view, is the capacity "to translate what she perceives in her own way, to link it to the unique intellectual adventure that makes her similar to all the rest in as much as this adventure is not like any other." This, Rancière concludes, "is the capacity of anonymous people, the capacity that makes everyone equal to everyone else."[49] The political critique of aesthetics, then, should not be focused on transforming spectators into actors, or vice versa. This just replays the binaries that make up the "stultifying" logic of subjection. For critique to overcome this logic, what is required is recognition of "the knowledge at work in the ignoramus and the activity peculiar to the spectator," as well as a "blurring of the boundary between those who act and those who look."[50]

When Levinas says that the subject is part of its own representation, he enacts the blurring of boundaries called for by Rancière. At the center of this blurring is the experience of rhythm, the force of sensation. Exposure to this rhythm involves the kind of suffering that comes with passivity, but it also opens up the possibilities that accompany any exploration of what is other than us, more powerful, unrepresentable, or unimaginable. Aesthetic experience, as a confrontation with the invisible forces of sensation, is not unlike a trial of strength that pushes us to outperform ourselves, or to perform in ways that we are incapable of imagining for ourselves. This, I think, is the promise of the aesthetic event that both Levinas and Deleuze describe as a horrific plunge into the night. Part of the horror of this descent is the horror that comes with any kind of experimentation with or exploration of the unknown. Nevertheless, it is a necessary step toward the extrication of oneself from oneself and necessary to escape the spectacular violence that would otherwise hold us captive.

Notes

1. Daniel Smith and Nathan Jun, eds., *Deleuze and Ethics* (Edinburgh: Edinburgh University Press, 2011).
2. In Merleau-Ponty's aesthetics there is a marked privileging of the synchronic relation between body and world, the senses and the sensed. Levinas, by contrast, pays more attention to the diachronic elements of aesthetics. See

Chapter 3 below for more on this.

3. Emmanuel Levinas, "Reality and Its Shadow," in *Collected Philosophical Papers*, trans. Alphonso Lingis (Pittsburgh: Duquesne University Press, 1987), 4.

4. Whereas Kant assigns a regulative function to reason, Hegel goes further in arguing that reason actively constitutes the objects of experience. See the discussion of reason in Tom Rockmore, *Cognition: An Introduction to Hegel's* Phenomenology of Spirit (Berkeley: University of California Press, 1997), 81.

5. Guy Debord, *The Society of the Spectacle*, trans. Donald Nicholson-Smith (New York: Zone Books, 1995), 15.

6. Throughout this essay I am leaving "art" intentionally vague because I am less interested in circumscribing the domain of art than I am in the way that every domain of experience involves an aesthetic aspect. In short, art is just one aesthetic domain that employs representations (as well as abstractions and affects) that bear on the body of the spectator.

7. Emmanuel Levinas, "Diachrony and Representation," in *Entre Nous: Thinking-of-the-Other*, trans. Michael B. Smith and Barbara Harshav (New York: Columbia University Press, 1998), 160.

8. Levinas, "Diachrony and Representation," 161.

9. Levinas, "Reality and Its Shadow," 3. In both German and French the terms used to describe conceptualizing, understanding, learning, and even perceiving refer us back to the acts of grasping or seizing hold. See Levinas's discussion in "Nonintentional Consciousness," in *Entre Nous*, 125-126.

10. See Levinas, "Reality and Its Shadow," 8. On delay as a form of "staggered time" in Deleuze and its contrast with the time theory of Bergson and Husserl, see Jay Lampert, *Simultaneity and Delay: A Dialectical Theory of Staggered Time* (London: Continuum, 2012).

11. Levinas, "Reality and Its Shadow," 3.

12. Levinas, "Reality and Its Shadow," 4.
13. Levinas, "Reality and Its Shadow," 3.
14. Levinas, "Reality and Its Shadow," 4.
15. See, for instance, Emmanuel Levinas, *Existence and Existents*, trans. Alphonso Lingis (Pittsburgh: Duquesne University Press, 1988), 80.
16. Levinas, "Reality and Its Shadow," 4.
17. Levinas, "Nonintentional Consciousness," 125.
18. Levinas, "Nonintentional Consciousness," 127-128.
19. Levinas, "Reality and Its Shadow," 3.
20. Levinas, *Existence and Existents*, 53.
21. Levinas, *Existence and Existents*, 47.
22. Levinas, *Existence and Existents*, 47.
23. Levinas, "Reality and Its Shadow," 5.
24. On this point, see Henri Bergson, *Matter and Memory*, trans. N.M. Paul and W.S. Palmer (New York: Zone Books, 1990). Bergson, it seems, is the liaison that links Levinas and Deleuze.
25. Levinas, "Reality and Its Shadow," 5.
26. Levinas, "Reality and Its Shadow," 5.
27. Gilles Deleuze, *Francis Bacon: The Logic of Sensation*, trans. Daniel Smith (Minneapolis: University of Minnesota Press, 2005), xxxii.
28. Levinas, "Nonintentional Consciousness," 124-125. See also Levinas's essay "Sensibility" in *Ontology and Alterity in Merleau-Ponty*, eds. Galen A. Johnson and Michael B. Smith (Evanston: Northwestern University Press, 1990), 65.
29. Deleuze, *Francis Bacon*, xxix.
30. Deleuze, *Francis Bacon*, xxxii.
31. Daniel Smith, "Translator's Introduction," in Deleuze, *Francis Bacon*, xv, xviii-xix.
32. Deleuze, *Francis Bacon*, 31.
33. Deleuze, *Francis Bacon*, 32.
34. Deleuze, *Francis Bacon*, 39.

35. Deleuze, *Francis Bacon*, 40.

36. Deleuze, *Francis Bacon*, 51.

37. Deleuze, *Francis Bacon*, 39.

38. See Levinas, *Existence and Existents*. Also note that the meaning and function of horror in Bacon's paintings, as seen by Deleuze, is different from the horror of the night described by Levinas. I have not explored this difference here.

39. This kind of violence is covered thoroughly in Susan Sontag, *Regarding the Pain of Others* (New York: Picador, 2004).

40. Deleuze, *Francis Bacon*, 36-37.

41. Deleuze, *Francis Bacon*, 52.

42. "Reality and Its Shadow," 6-8. Where Levinas differs from Deleuze is over the role of meaning in spectatorship. Levinas insists that even in nonintentional consciousness, or what Deleuze might call asignifying experience, there is *meaning*. See Levinas, "Nonintentional Consciousness," 124.

43. Jacque Rancière, *The Emancipated Spectator*, trans. Gregory Elliott (London: Verso, 2009), 2.

44. See the discussion of insomnia in Levinas, *Existence and Existents*, 61-64 and Chapter 2 above.

45. For more on the nature of caricature and withdrawal, see the work of Graham Harman, which gathers some of its inspiration from Levinas.

46. Rancière, *The Emancipated Spectator*, 12. On the meaning of the "distribution of the sensible" and Rancière's affinity with Deleuze on the question of sensation, see Davide Panagia, *The Political Life of Sensation* (Durham: Duke University Press, 2009), chapter 1.

47. Rancière, *The Emancipated Spectator*, 13.

48. Rancière, *The Emancipated Spectator*, 15.

49. Rancière, *The Emancipated Spectator*, 16-17.

50. Rancière, *The Emancipated Spectator*, 17, 19.

3

Aesthetic Identity[1]

Introduction

Among those interested in the history of phenomenology, and the work of Maurice Merleau-Ponty in particular, it is common knowledge that the phenomenology of the body articulated in *Phenomenology of Perception* owes an incredible debt to Edmund Husserl's second volume of *Ideas*.[2] This is the book where Husserl talks at length about the body. The themes of bodily kinaesthetics and motility, operative intentionality, passive synthesis—distinctly corporeal acts in Merleau-Ponty's work— are all taken up from Husserl's analyses. Merleau-Ponty's memorial essay "The Philosopher and His Shadow" testifies to this debt. Even the theme I take up in this chapter, what Merleau-Ponty calls the "ontological rehabilitation of the sensible," is credited to Husserl.[3] Levinas spearheads this rehabilitation no less than Merleau-Ponty.

Despite the depth of his reliance on Husserl, Merleau-Ponty's phenomenology of the body manages to establish a claim that is, at most, dormant in his predecessor's research into embodiment. This is the claim that *I am my body*. Merleau-Ponty's original contribution to phenomenology, if not philosophy, is "the thesis that I am my body; that I am a subjective object or a physical subject."[4] Thus, Merleau-Ponty's corporeal phenomenology aspires to evacuate the interiority of personal identity by rendering the interior/exterior distinction false and replacing it in the end with the notion of "flesh" (*la chair*). Flesh is the term he will use to denote the essential identity of body and world and to indicate that subject and object, seer and seen, are cut from the same cloth. This identification effectively reduces personal identity to bodily identity. This is, to be sure, a complex (meta)physical form of identity, one which considers the body as a complex sensible event, or a "haecceity of Nature." The notion of haecceity is employed by Deleuze (and Guattari) in a number of places, including *A Thousand Plateaus*. Deleuze and Guattari describe a haecceity as an "accidental form," and thereby designate an individual body—in cartographic terms—as "the sum total of the material elements belonging to it under given relations of movement and rest, speed and slowness (longitude); the sum total of the intensive affects it is capable of at a given power or degree of potential (latitude)."[5] While similar to Deleuze and Guattari's understanding, Merleau-Ponty does not quite affirm the accidental character of corporeal form—his idea of bodily identity remains bound to the ends of human projects, and is thus informed by the teleology of human perception.

The reduction of personal identity in Merleau-Ponty's phenomenology is an extremely rich reduction: it leaves room for self-awareness, reflection, and a positive understanding of freedom. His reduced identity is constituted at the basic level by intentionality, the body schema, and the aggregate of acquired habits that enable the body to cope in the practical world.[6] But it is also constituted by what Merleau-Ponty calls sense experience (*le sentir*) and sensation (*sensation*), two different but related terms at play in his text. It is at this level that the body is animated by its "communion"[7] with the world and it is at this level that the body leads its "anonymous"[8] existence, a life whose experiences are never presented to perception. The body's anonymous existence is formed by what Merleau-Ponty calls "a past which has never been present." This past names the pre-perceptual *aesthetic* life of the body.[9] In the last analysis, however, Merleau-Ponty invokes a distinction between the divergent multiplicity of sensations and the unifying activity of perception without following up on the challenges that such a distinction poses to his "primacy of perception" thesis, a thesis that commits him to the view that the convergence of perception, which draws together and tames the "unstable" and "alien" events of sensation, takes precedence over sensation's divergent force.[10] This is a consequence of his allegiance to the phenomenological method, which effectively bypasses ("brackets") the metaphysics of sensation, or transubstantiates sensation into "hyletic data."[11] Phenomenology eludes a direct confrontation with the materiality of sensation.

It is not surprising that Merleau-Ponty would hesitate to give pride of place to sensation in his ontology of the body. Sensation is a term endorsed by outdated empiricists and positivists like Ernst Mach,[12] while phenomenology defines itself in part by its opposition to positivism, behaviorism, and the like. The *Phenomenology of Perception* opens with a critique of the concept of sensation, which is summed up when Merleau-Ponty states that a pure sensation "corresponds to nothing in our experience."[13] Sensation is always mingled with perception and therefore inseparable from the operations of perception described throughout the *Phenomenology*. By championing perception over sensation Merleau-Ponty aims to mark his distance from eliminativist and positivist accounts of embodiment, and to render inoperative or derivative the vocabularies of competing theories of behavior and embodiment. After his position is established, however, Merleau-Ponty will once again take up the question of sensation and ask us to regard it anew through the lens of perception. In a more direct manner Levinas makes a case for the irreducible affective significance of sensation.

I will not explore here the methodological and metaphysical problems involved in the phenomenological engagement with sensation, for surely they exist even when the phenomenologist is reluctant to thematize them. Instead I want to indicate a few of the positive ways that Levinas and Merleau-Ponty help us understand the aesthetic life of the body. It seems to me that their philosophies give us a prototypical understanding of corporeal *plasticity*, and make significant contributions to the rehabilitation of sensation as a viable philosophical concept. It is sensation that gives us our material link to the world; it provides a means for grounding identity in the environment and understanding the ways our sensory environments can hinder or promote our well-being. A rich conception of the ambivalence of sensation is therefore needed to understand the body's embeddedness in and dependence on the environment, as well as its identity as an aesthetic object. Once this conception of sensation is clear, I will briefly outline how it contributes to environmental ethics.

I use the term *integrity* to denote the identity of the body and to emphasize the quality of its structure. So when I use this term I do not mean it in the moral sense, but in the sense intended when someone says, "The integrity of the building has been compromised by the earthquake." The analogy between bodies and buildings is drawn deliberately here. And this is not just for the sake of analogy, but so I can eventually suggest the reciprocal determination of bodies and buildings. However, I also wish to emphasize that a body's integrity, as well as what I call its plasticity, is not entirely determinable by its relations. Plasticity and integrity are internal to the body qua body as long as it exists as an individual, although the duration of its existence as *this* or *that* individual (i.e., haecceity) depends upon the relations it enters into. Thus bodies can be regarded as autonomous, but this by no means commits us to the view that there is something about their individuality that is immune to external influence. The body's integrity and plasticity are both capable of being compromised to the point of annihilation or irreversible automatism, which amount to the same thing. The idea of plasticity helps us think of autonomy beyond the freedom/determinism dichotomy by showing that our susceptibility to influence is what allows us to acquire a structure upon which to act upon, react to, or resist influence.

Before articulating my position on aesthetic identity, I want to say a few things by way of contrast about Kant's aesthetics.

Kant's Aesthetics

The British empiricists who influenced and provoked Kant's philosophy were not afraid to speak about sensations and the effect they have on our minds. Locke, Berkeley, and Hume, of course, spoke like this, as did Francis Hutcheson. Hutcheson writes that, "Those Ideas which are rais'd in the Mind upon the presence of external Objects, and their acting upon our Bodys, are call'd Sensations." He continues: "We find that the Mind in such Cases is passive, and has not Power directly to prevent the Perception or Idea, or to vary it at its Reception, as long as we continue our Bodys in a state fit to be acted upon by the external Object."[14] Despite the fact that he refers to them as "ideas" (like Berkeley) Hutcheson ascribes the delivery of sensations to external objects (unlike Berkeley). Sensations are objectively given: they are *real*, not merely epiphenomenal byproducts.

Kant, who was influenced by Hutcheson, holds a parallel view of sensation. Kant writes in the Transcendental Aesthetic of his *Critique of Pure Reason*: "The effect of an object on our capacity for [re]presentation, insofar as we are affected by the object, is *sensation*."[15] For Kant, sensation furnishes the material that the understanding fashions into experience; but it is never apprehended in its pure manifoldness. Since we begin our critical inquiry into the origin of knowledge from organized experience, we can only ever work backward to the disorganization of sensation. That is, we can only *infer* that formless sensations are given to the understanding. This is how the transcendental method works. But if sensation, for Kant, is always already worked up into a representation by our cognitive faculty, then what allows him to claim that something like a pure manifold of sensation actually exists? As Merleau-Ponty points out, we never experience anything of the sort. Kant's picture of cognition requires the concept of sensation, or the sensory manifold, to account for the content of cognition. But beyond its basic architectonic/formal value sensation plays no formative role in the constitution of experience or identity; nor does it hold sway over our capacity to constitute experience.[16] In short, Kant's transcendental aesthetic idealizes sensation and thereby severs the link — maintained by his predecessor Baumgarten — between the mind and the material world.

There is, of course, a practical purpose to Kant's Transcendental Aesthetic. He ensures that the material world and its volatile multiplicity of sensations remain at an infinite remove from the transcendental ego which signifies the locus of personal identity and the seat of human freedom. Ontologically speaking, a gap exists between the transcendental subject and the world of things. The body of the subject consequently is left out of Kant's theory of identity, as Merleau-Ponty does not fail to note in the *Phenomenology*.[17] No matter what happens to the body in the physical world, the real identity of the subject is untouched; its freedom is quite immune to the laws of nature and natural events.[18] This means that, as Samuel Todes puts it, Kant "has no sense of how practice *makes* the practitioner."[19] The price Kant must pay for protecting the freedom of the subject is that he cannot account for how the material of the practical world shapes who we are as individuals.

Angelica Nuzzo has argued that Kant does not in fact leave the body out of his equation. If we look to the *Critique of Judgment*, for instance, we see the embodied dimension of sensibility highlighted by Kant. The experiences of pleasure and displeasure in the face of aesthetic phenomena allow us to "*feel* ourselves a part of living (i.e., sensible) nature."[20] She concludes that "[Kant's] general aim is to attribute to human sensibility a new central place in philosophy, thereby steering the philosophical focus from the metaphysics of a 'disembodied soul' to the inquiry into an 'embodied mind'." Kant's modern view of sensibility is broad enough to encompass "the entire realm of the sensual:

affections, intuition, sensation, feeling, and imagination."[21] The innovative moment in Kant arrives when he makes the body a transcendental condition for aesthetics, a condition which is both "formal" and "ideal," but at the same time corporeal.

In her recent book *Ideal Embodiment* Nuzzo contends that Kant's theory of sensibility is ultimately a theory of *embodied* sensibility and that, "Transcendentally, the knowing subject of Kant's epistemology, the moral agent of his pure ethics, and the evaluating subject of his aesthetic theory of judgment is a rational embodied being."[22] The transcendental dimension of embodiment is exemplified in the fact that perception is governed, a priori, by a left/right asymmetry that corresponds to the asymmetry of our hands. In short, the a priori form of space (the formal aspect of sensible intuition) has left and right built into it.[23] This asymmetry is not merely physical: it is a transcendental condition of any possible experience.

I would not dispute the existence of a transcendental embodiment in Kant, for Nuzzo's position is both thorough and compelling. It does not, however, succeed in reuniting the body of the subject to the material world. In fact, her argument explicitly resists such a reunion. As a result, the Kantian subject's identity remains beyond the reach of other bodies. And, moreover, those bodies must always be seen as themselves constituted by the subject's sensibility and understanding. This entails (1) the impossibility of the subject's identity being either formed or deformed by sensation and (2) a reduction of the otherness of the environment.

As everyone knows, Levinas's entire ethical critique of the history of philosophy works against such a reduction. But instead of following that line of thinking here I will discuss the way Levinas's aesthetics reinforces the immanence of subject and object by advocating the constitutive function of sensation.

Proto-Plasticity in Carnal Phenomenology

Perhaps Levinas's most challenging book is *Otherwise than Being*, wherein he undertakes a sustained deconstruction of sensibility that tacitly engages and operates against the more formal account of Kant. The aim of Levinas's analysis is to show that, "Even when unformed, or deformed, by knowing, sensible intuition can revert to its own meaning."[24] In large measure Levinas's argument is an attempt to relocate outside the subject the origin of the world's animation. That is, against Kant, he wants us to see that experience is animated by the difference introduced by the other and not by the synthetic activity of our minds. The relation of our "animate body" or "incarnate identity," as he calls it, "can be understood as an exposure to the other, the passivity of the for-the-other in vulnerability, which refers to maternity, which sensibility signifies."[25] Sensibility is neither activity nor the mere receptivity of preformed representations. Sensibility, the site of sensation, is the place where the identity of the world and the identity of my body come to pass simultaneously, yet diachronically.

Levinas's account of embodiment in *Otherwise than Being*, however, ends up overstressing the susceptibility of the body in the face of the sensible environment. His incarnate subject remains hyperbolically vulnerable to the sensations of the other, its skin invariably exposed to both solicited and unsolicited touching. An entire vocabulary testifies to this inescapable susceptibility:

> Vulnerability, exposure to outrage, to wounding, passivity more passive than all patience...trauma of accusation suffered by a hostage to the point of persecution, implicating the identity of the hostage who substitutes himself for the others; all this is the self, a defecting or defeat of the ego's identity. And this, pushed to the limit, is sensibility, sensibility as the subjectivity of the subject.[26]

Levinas shifts sensibility and, by consequence, sensation to the center of our thinking about identity. The skin acts as the edge or boundary between subject and world (although this distinction is simply verbal). As Rudolf Bernet explains,

> Even a tight and thick skin has small and large holes that one can adequately call "openings." There are natural openings as well as artificial or forced openings called "wounds." Natural openings are still subject, however, to being forced and wounded. The natural openings allowing for a passage and exchange between the inside and the outside of a body cannot prevent the violence of a traumatic intrusion or expulsion.[27]

The collapse of subject and object, inside and outside, into the operations of sensibility effectuates a perpetual "breakup of identity"[28] by turning identity into little more than an *event* of sensibility. The constancy of sensation and our inability to cease the influx of sensible material puts us constantly at risk of having our familiar experiences disfigured, our bodies disabled. This, as I indicated in the previous chapter, is what Deleuze has in mind when he writes in his book on Francis Bacon that "sensation is the master of deformations, the agent of bodily deformations."[29] That sensation animates us, instead of us animating it, is part of what Deleuze calls the "logic of sensation." This he shares with Levinas.

Although in the final analysis vulnerability is the defining feature of sensibility for Levinas, it is also a site of what he calls *alimentation*. Sensations are not only what threaten to break up identities, they are also what nourish identities. Our bodies metabolize sensations and thereby incorporate them into their constitution. Conversely, bodies excrete sensations back into the environment. Bodies soak up and radiate aesthetics. Just as there is a vocabulary of susceptibility in Levinas's later work, there is a whole vocabulary of alimentation to be found especially in

Totality and Infinity. This vocabulary includes the notions of "living from…," "enjoyment," "fecundity," "satisfaction," and "habitation." The consumption of food is simply the most mundane type of alimentation. Levinas uses it as a general term for the process of identity-constitution. Love, joy, and work for Levinas nourish us just as much as bread or water. The alimentary is nourishment and a source of enjoyment, and it is precisely our enjoyment, or affectivity more generally, which effects our separation from undifferentiated existence—being qua being, the sensible as such—and makes us ecstatic,[30] autonomous agents. Our affective life enacts the principle of our individuation, makes us practitioners in Todes's sense. Levinas writes:

> One does not only exist one's pain or one's joy; one exists from pains and joys. Enjoyment is precisely this way the act nourishes itself with its own activity. To live from bread is therefore neither to represent bread to oneself nor to act on it nor to act by means of it. To be sure, it is necessary to earn one's bread, and it is necessary to nourish oneself in order to earn one's bread; thus the bread I eat is also that with which I earn my bread and my life. But if I eat my bread in order to labor and to live, I live *from* my labor and *from* my bread.[31]

In other words, only after we have been affected do we become animated individuals adept at manipulating things and working toward future projects. "Subjectivity," writes Levinas, "originates in the independence and sovereignty of enjoyment."[32] Perhaps with a critical glance at Merleau-Ponty and Heidegger, Levinas here makes affectivity a transcendental condition of practical life.

It must be kept in mind that our "sovereign" and "independent" affective life is *incited* by the other, nourished by the sensations bestowed upon our sensibility by other bodies. Affectivity is not autoaffection, but alimentation:

Nourishment, as a means of invigoration, is the transmu-
tation of the other into the same, which is in the essence of
enjoyment: an energy that is other, recognized as other, recognized...as sustaining the very act that is directed upon it,
becomes, in enjoyment, my own energy, my strength, me. All
enjoyment is in this sense alimentation.[33]

The enjoyment we derive from breathing comes from the other;
we live as individuals because the other is there to inhale and
exhale. As Silvia Benso has said, the activity of breathing is "an
animation [that] does not occur at the level of cognition, theory,
or intentionality" but "is only possible at the level of the body,
through an incarnation."[34] On this reading the integral form of
the subject is not imposed via the incarnation of a soul, it is
generated through an exchange of material. It is what Hans Jonas
has called *metabolism*: through the metabolic process, the organic
body trades its matter with the matter of its surroundings. This
exchange gives rise to a "living form" whose matter is never the
same, but which nevertheless retains a certain integrity.[35] And as
with Levinas's alimentation, this exchange of material need not
be an organic process. Inorganic material, even sensations, can
provide nourishment for organisms.

Levinas would have us imagine this vitality as an event of
generation that is variously described as a "coiling," "folding
back," "spiral," and "involution."[36] The language here is meant
to denote the immanent constitution of the individual and the
event-like structure of the subject's integrity. The subject is
produced as an "eddy"[37] of affectivity; it maintains its integrity
as long as its common sources of joy or pain affect it.
Uncommon, overwhelming, or traumatic affects/sensations
threaten to form it into something quite different. The substance
of the self is then little more than the viscosity or consistency of
its sensuous life, or a finite expression of the sensible.[38] I would
call this kind of substance "plastic" in order to draw attention to

its event-like structure and its indeterminate, fluid capacity to take on and release form. I will retrieve this Levinasian insight, and say more about plasticity, below.

There is a complementary and more popular view of embodied subjectivity found in Merleau-Ponty. The work of sensation in Merleau-Ponty's view is often subsumed into his theory of perception, however. He advances a "new status for sensation," attributing to it a "motor physiognomy" and a "living significance."[39] Sensations are neither mental content nor sense data nor stimuli. Sensations are transmitted to the body in its dialogue with objects and awaken its sensorium, bringing it to life. They are, in a strong sense, its vitality. Lest we conclude that the body is at the mercy of the sensible environment, however, he repeatedly refers to sensation as a *power* (*puissance*) of the body, one which is "synchronized" with the "existential environment."[40] This point is consonant with his transactional view of subject/world relations as well as its more radical expression, the doctrine of the flesh.[41] Significantly for my argument, this power is determined by the singular array of perspectives any individual body embodies, and the range of corresponding appearances that attend this set of perspectives.[42] Power is determined by the totality of aesthetic experiences a body takes in. As Alphonso Lingis puts it, "The sensitive body is the locus of inscription of inner postural axes on external visibility and of external visibility on its inner postural diagram."[43] Consequently, knowing *how* precisely my body is determined—or, put otherwise, knowing how to locate my longitude and latitude—*is* my freedom and my power. This know-how Merleau-Ponty calls "praktognosia," a kind of perceptual and practical competence.[44] This is entailed in Merleau-Ponty's claim that "consciousness is in the first place not a matter of 'I think that' but of 'I can'."[45] This I take to be a Spinozist sentiment, with the difference that for Merleau-Ponty it is the habituated body that knows, not the intellect.

There are a number of places in Merleau-Ponty's work where he shows a commitment to the body's plasticity, where he understands its integrity as both indefinitely formable and formative of identity. In his discussion of the habit body and the body schema, for instance, he clearly wants us to regard the body's identity as dialogically constituted and open-ended. As with Levinas this identity is aggregated and defined by an indeterminate capacity to act and be acted upon. He refers to the body at one point in the *Phenomenology* as "a mosaic of sensations" with "no specific direction."[46] This indeterminacy is marked by a threshold, or the absence of a specific locus of identity. Not unlike Hume's stageless theatre of personal identity, Berkeley's Lockean definition of the object as a collection of qualities,[47] or the Levinasian subject outlined above, Merleau-Ponty's mosaic body has no immutable core. It is, in short, "a fold, which has been made and which can be unmade."[48] What Deleuze writes about Hume applies *for the most part* to Merleau-Ponty: "The place is not different from what takes place in it; the representation does not take place *in* a subject."[49]

No one will deny that there are numerous incompatibilities between the authors referenced in the last paragraph. Nevertheless they display a common commitment to thinking the insubstantiality of the subject (or the object, in Berkeley's case), *without* allowing this subject to be completely dispersed into an impersonal field of forces. This effort I take to be commensurate with the theory of plastic subjectivity. The plastic subject is a dispositional subject, transitory and mutable. Its disposition is informed by its sensory environments and discernible in the sensations it can endure and produce at any given moment. If the identity of the body is marked by a threshold for Merleau-Ponty—a threshold for practical action dictated by the existential environment, the body's habits, and the appearances delimiting its singular perspective—I take this threshold to be plastic in the sense William James intends when he defines plasticity as "the possession of a structure weak enough to yield to an influence, but strong enough not to yield all at once." [50] Under this definition corporeal integrity is a matter of degree and is never precisely fixed. Integrity will be reinforced or compromised by the aesthetic environment and the entire range of sensory encounters it engenders, from personal communication device interfaces to urban greenways, from airport terminal acoustics to the building materials and lighting of Kiasma in Helsinki.

The threshold of identity is explored at length in Merleau-Ponty's treatment of painting, particularly the work of Cézanne. He explicitly draws an analogy between the body and the work of art which enables us to understand what he takes corporeal identity to be.[51] "For each object," Merleau-Ponty writes, "as for each picture in an art gallery, there is an optimum distance from which it requires to be seen."[52] Between the body and the work of art there lies a privileged perceptual position that reveals the true identity of the work. This position allows me to "identify the object [or painting] in all its positions, at all distances, in all appearances, insofar as all the perspectives converge towards the perception which I obtain at a certain distance and with a certain typical orientation."[53] Of course the position at which a painting's identity appears is not exact, but variable to a degree. Its variability, however, can devolve into the obliteration of the painting's identity. Move too far away from the painting and you lose clarity. At the extreme it disappears completely from sight. The identity of a work of art is thus determined by an "ideal limit," a threshold which dictates how close is too close and how far is too far for perceiving it. This ideal limit is studied in Cézanne's painting, which is why his objects often appear on the verge of losing their integrity.[54] If the body is like a work of art, a mosaic in particular, then its integrity will admit of a set of limits beyond which it ceases to be *this* body and becomes another body altogether. There will be no substantial core underlying its aesthetic variation; within that set of limits it will retain its integrity (or form or clarity) even if some components are added or removed.[55] This is what is means to be a plastic body.

Nourishing Spaces

If the integrity of the body depends on the aggregate of sensations it receives, then the spaces it inhabits (to take just one example of an aesthetic environment) are an essential constituent of its identity. Spaces, too—whether natural or built—offer a source of alimentation, their own unique sensory mosaic. Presumably we want to cultivate spaces that enable rather than disable our bodies. In the case of built spaces we want their integrity to at a minimum reinforce and, ideally, promote or augment our integrity.[56] An architectural philosophy whose buildings seek primarily to adapt to the human body, or which takes the reality of space to be a product of intentional perceptual syntheses, is inadequate from an ecological perspective, and not least of all because it is anthropocentric. Further, we want to avoid habitats that compromise us by pushing the tolerance of our plasticity beyond its breaking point. From the standpoint of plasticity this breakage is the very meaning of death. We will then want to multiply the habitats that increase our capacity to affect and be affected, that is, increase our power to exist. For this to occur environmental aesthetics and architecture must confront the plasticity of the body. Can a phenomenological aesthetics accomplish this? Not if it neglects the materiality of sensation.

Edward Casey, following Merleau-Ponty (and implicitly Bourdieu), defines a habitat as a familiar kinaesthetic situation, one which gives rise to a practical aptitude required for orienting oneself in the environment. In a habitat, he writes, "we can be 'ethical' in the originary sense of the word, which implies a community of like-minded (but not necessarily like-bodied) creatures."[57] Habitats sustain us and offer us the opportunity to cultivate ourselves as long as we are willing and able to meet their demands. When we do they enable in us a certain set of dispositions for action. This "power of orientation," or *habitus*, dictates what we can and cannot do.[58] Insofar as a *habitus* is the internalization of a habitat, the structure of the body exemplifies and expresses the structure of the habitat. And this is not because the body is flexible or adaptable, but because it is plastic: it can fashion its habitat, and therefore its *habitus*, just as much as it is fashioned by it.[59] A neglect or careless cultivation of the habitat risks violating its integrity and, consequently, endangering that of our bodies.

Architectural theorists attuned to the phenomenology of the body foreground the body's reflection of its environment. Peter Zumthor speaks of the "atmosphere" of built spaces and how our "emotional sensibility," rather than our sense perception or judgment, apprehends it.[60] Architecture, for Zumthor, is about how atmosphere embraces the bodies dwelling within it. He writes:

> It's like our own bodies with their anatomy and things we can't see and skin covering us — that's what architecture means to me and that's how I try to think about it. As a bodily mass, a membrane, a fabric, a kind of covering, cloth, velvet, silk, all around me. The body! Not the idea of the body — the body itself! A body that can touch me.[61]

In a similar vein, Juhani Pallasmaa writes of how our bodies assume atmospheres in their skeletal and sensory infrastructure. This infrastructure is first embodied in the architect, then transmitted into the body of the inhabitants.[62] Such a transmission is possible, I would contend, because the body is plastic, susceptible to spatial aesthetics but also capable of apprehending the power embedded in any space that does not compromise its integrity. The creative aspect of the plastic body is its capacity to stylize this power into new buildings it can then integrate into itself. My contention is that these body/building transactions occur first and foremost at the impersonal, non-phenomenal level of sensation. This level is non-intentional and with "no specific direction," as Merleau-Ponty admits. This means that aesthetic design cannot be content with the data provided by perception. Perception cannot fully predict how an environment will affect the senses, nor can it know which environments will enhance or diminish the body's power. In a sense these events will happen by chance. Phenomenology, for all its promise, has trouble handling the non-phenomenal and the non-intentional. This is precisely because phenomenality and intentionality are the fundamental elements of its understanding of experience. As Pallasmaa ultimately puts it, "the generative force [of the body and the building] lies in the intentions."[63]

As if despite their allegiance to phenomenological principles Levinas and Merleau-Ponty make valuable contributions to the rehabilitation of sensation as a concept. But these contributions oftentimes seem in tension with the first-person perspective of phenomenology, assuming instead the form of metaphysical speculation on the genesis of subjectivity and the materiality of the sensible realm. Such speculation is without question required for a complete understanding of corporeal identity. Without it we are left only with description. Design, architectural and otherwise, needs more than description if it is going to realize the unforeseen power of bodies.

Let me illustrate an earlier point: our habitat is reflected in our *habitus*. We may recall the habits taken on by Thoreau at Walden Pond. Only a certain set of habits were available to him if he desired to be shaped by that unique habitat called Walden. A balance had to be struck between his efforts at cultivation, on the one hand, and his yielding to the environment, on the other, in order to preserve his integrity along with Walden's.[64] He could till the land, but not so much that its fertility would be diminished. He could last the winter, but only if the season's conditions did not exceed his fortitude. We might imagine Walden and consider the unique set of sensations that make up its aesthetic identity, as well as the sensations put into that habitat by Thoreau himself.[65] It could be said that, in a strong sense, Thoreau *became* Walden while living there, that Thoreau would not be Thoreau had he not inhabited that space. But what would Walden have become if Thoreau failed to respect its integrity? Imagine the sensations that would result if the threshold separating and uniting Thoreau and Walden were compromised by either of them.

The relation of body and environment is not always harmonious, however. Indeed, it is often, if not always, *volatile.* Sensations, as Merleau-Ponty teaches, are the unstable, the alien. They are alimentary, on the one hand, but on the other they threaten always to break us up. Given the volatility of sensation and the plasticity of our identities we need an ethical principle that will tell us what kind of environments we should endorse. Architect Michael Benedikt offers a useful definition of value to accompany the aesthetics of embodiment sketched so far. He says: "'positive value' is what we attribute to that which intensifies and/or prolongs life. Conversely, 'negative value' is what we attribute to that which dilutes and/or shortens life."[66] This again is a sentiment very close to Spinoza.

Benedikt acknowledges the anthropocentrism at work in his definition, but nothing prevents us from applying it to existence in general. The point is to increase power and proliferate the possibilities of existence wherever we can, whether we are constructing or building or restoring or conserving. But whose power? Ideally any creature capable of giving and receiving sensations. Does this exclude inanimate objects? Not necessarily, for they too belong to the aesthetic economy and participate in the intensification and prolongation of "life" understood as an integrated sensory system. The obvious obstacle here is adjudicating situations where power needs to be sacrificed in the name of some other end, but this problem must be deferred for now.

Spinozist Aesthetics and the Future of Plasticity

It is rare to find two figures more committed to the renewal of sensation after Kant than Merleau-Ponty and Levinas. I have tried to indicate some of the ways they can enrich our understanding of sensation, but I have also raised some concerns about the usefulness of phenomenology's approach to embodiment and environmental aesthetics. Its anthropocentric perspective may very well do justice to the richness and complexity of human existence, but its descriptions of spatiality and aesthetic experience must always refer back to the intentionality of the subject. It is true that this subject is seen as embedded and situated in a concrete environment, but this concreteness is always informed by the teleological practice of the subject. Consequently the existential features of the lifeworld are privileged over the material, and the embodied subject is regarded as relatively free to transcend its situation. But an existential situation is not a material environment. Their dynamics are quite different. An environmental aesthetics or architectural theory driven by the phenomenologist's picture of embodiment will accommodate the body as lived, existential project, but it will do so at the neglect of the material basis of aesthetic identity.

Although they are amenable to plasticity it is not necessary to return to the phenomenologists to advance the concept. Indeed, I have suggested that the metaphysics of phenomenology restricts a complete commitment to the plastic body. Nor is it necessary to go to Deleuze, or even James, as I have done here, to find the concept at work in the history of philosophy. Plasticity is operative in prototypical form in most "anti-essentialist" approaches to human nature, embodiment, and personal identity. Catherine Malabou has recently found the concept in Hegel and taken up research in neuroscience with a view to developing a politics of plasticity.[67] Neuroplasticity has become an indispensable idea for contemporary brain scientists; it is the empirical equivalent of the plasticity we find in James's speculative neurology. For my part I would argue that the philosophy of the body we find in Spinoza is centered on the concept of plasticity and preferable to the phenomenological body for several reasons.

First, Spinoza's monistic ontology considers bodies as expressions of a single substance, rather than as individual loci of perception or consciousness. Human beings hold no privileged position in the constitution of experience or the environment, which means they are no more capable of transcending the events of the material world than any other bodies. This leveling of the field of being to a single plane of nature has a democratic edge to it, eliminating the distinction between human and nonhuman, natural and artificial, and the hierarchy of beings. Second, instead of regarding the immanence of nature as the absence of freedom, he shows us how to see our determination as our freedom: our power to exist is based on nothing other than the way we are determined by our material conditions, our precise longitude and latitude. Third, consciousness, intentionality, and interiority are left out of the picture of embodiment; we must think the body and its embeddedness in their materiality alone. Everything the body can do must be accounted for in terms of "corporeal surfaces, in terms of rotations, convolutions, inflections, and torsions of the body itself."[68] Reducing the body to its surface (immanent) identity obliges us to shift our attention to its aesthetic relations.

For Spinoza a body is never a pure individual. It is always a composite, an aggregate or ecology of bodies working together *as* an individual. Some human bodies in a building or in the street can unite to form a individual; several animal and inanimate bodies can unite to form an individual; some furniture, paintings, and lighting fixtures can unite to form an individual, or they may fail to do so. It all depends on how the surfaces affect each other and the effect produced. An individual is a material effect, not a perceptual phenomenon, with an identity determined by its singular disposition, that is, its power to affect and be affected.[69] This formula names the plasticity of the Spinozist body. Its power is formally variable, which means that some of the bodies in the composite can be substituted or eliminated, as long as the composite's effect remains intact. From a practical point of view the body's identity is gleaned by asking, *What can the body do?* Or, *What is its pain and pleasure threshold?* To answer these questions we need to know which sensations the body can endure and which sensations the body can exhibit. This is the task of design teams, whether in the domain of art, architecture, virtual environments, or urban planning. If we do not know what a body can do, then we must actively pursue, by design, the power of the unperceivable and unpredictable. A Dionysian ethic of exposure and non-censorship suggests itself: "Dionysus affirms all that appears...and appears in all that is affirmed."[70] A fully worked out a Spinozist aesthetics can help us embrace this principle.[71] Spinoza's philosophy has already had a significant impact on the deep ecology movement, but I think he should be enlisted in the *shallow ecology* of Levinas and Merleau-Ponty. I suspect his contribution to architecture would not be insignificant.[72] In sum, his promise lies in his plastic conception of embodiment, his materialist framework, as well as his democratic theory of bodies and environmental relations.[73] His philosophy affirms the equality of bodies, the advantage of cultivating convivial ecological habits, and an equitable distribution of power, all of which are at stake in environmental ethics and political ecology.

Notes

1. This chapter originally appeared as "Plasticity and Aesthetic Identity; or, Why We Need a Spinozist Aesthetics" in *The*

Nordic Journal of Aesthetics 40/41 (2011): 53-74.

2.   Edmund Husserl, *Ideas Pertaining to a Pure Phenomenology and to a Phenomenological Philosophy*, second book, trans. Richard Rojcewicz and Andre Schuwer (Dordrecht; Springer, 1990).

3.   Maurice Merleau-Ponty, "The Philosopher and His Shadow," in *Signs*, trans. Richard C. McCleary (Evanston: Northwestern University Press, 1964), 167.

4.   Stephen Priest, *Merleau-Ponty* (London: Routledge, 1998), 57.

5.   Merleau-Ponty, "The Philosopher and His Shadow," 165.

6.   See Maurice Merleau-Ponty, *Phenomenology of Perception*, trans. Colin Smith (London: Routledge and Kegan Paul, 1962), 142-143.

7.   Merleau-Ponty, *Phenomenology of Perception*, 212.

8.   On anonymity, see *Phenomenology of Perception*, 215. In this vein we could invoke the autonomic nervous system as a primary dimension of the body which functions for the most part below the level of consciousness. From the perspective of phenomenology this system must remain anonymous, never present directly as a phenomenon.

9.   See *Phenomenology of Perception*, 242, and Alia Al-Saji, "'A Past Which Has Never Been Present': Bergsonian Dimensions in Merleau-Ponty's Theory of the Prepersonal," *Research in Phenomenology* 38 (2008): 41-71. Since sensation belongs always to the past, we might say that it exists virtually (which is not to say merely potentially). Its effects are always actualized, but never present to perception, which remains directed on the future. Note that I am using "aesthetic" here in a broad sense to refer to the sensory environment writ large.

10. See Merleau-Ponty, *Phenomenology of Perception*, 230.

11. See §36 of Edmund Husserl, *Ideas*, trans. W.R. Boyce Gibson (New York: Collier, 1962), where Husserl makes sensation (now termed "hyletic data") fully *immanent to* consciousness, thus attenuating, if not negating, its externality.

12. See Ernst Mach, *The Analysis of Sensations*, trans. C.M. Williams and Sydney Waterlow (New York: Dover, 1959).

13. Merleau-Ponty, *Phenomenology of Perception*, 3.

14. Quoted in Davide Panagia, *The Political Life of Sensation* (Durham: Duke University Press, 2009), 24.

15. Immanuel Kant, *Critique of Pure Reason*, trans. Werner S. Pluhar (Indianapolis: Hackett, 1996), B34/A20.

16. Furthermore, he is not entitled to Hutcheson's claim that objects *cause* sensations in us. Causality occurs only in the phenomenal world; Kant cannot maintain that noumenal entities impress themselves upon us, thus inciting the mind to activity. This is originally, I believe, Maimon's objection.

17. Merleau-Ponty, *Phenomenology of Perception*, 303.

18. The view that human freedom is beyond the reach of nature—namely, that human and natural laws are completely independent of one another—is glimpsed when Kant writes in the third *Critique*: "The great gulf that separates the supersensible from appearances completely cuts off the domain of the concept of nature under the one legislation, and the domain of the concept of freedom under the other legislation, from any influence that each (according to its own basic laws) might have had on the other." Immanuel Kant, *Critique of Judgment*, trans. Werner S. Pluhar (Indianapolis: Hackett, 1987), Introduction, IX, 195.

19. Samuel Todes, *Body and World* (Cambridge, MA: MIT Press, 2001), 173, my emphasis.

20. Angelica Nuzzo, "Kant and Herder on Baumgarten's *Aesthetica*," *Journal of the History of Philosophy* 44, no. 4 (October 2006): 587.

21. "Kant and Herder," 578.

22. Angelica Nuzzo, *Ideal Embodiment: Kant's Theory of Sensibility* (Bloomington: Indiana University Press, 2008), 5.

23. Nuzzo, *Ideal Embodiment*, 10-11.

24. Emmanuel Levinas, *Otherwise than Being; or, Beyond Essence*,

trans. Alphonso Lingis (Pittsburgh: Duquesne University Press, 1997), 63.

25. Levinas, *Otherwise than Being*, 71.

26. Levinas, *Otherwise than Being*, 15.

27. Rudolf Bernet, "The Encounter with the Stranger: Two Interpretations of the Vulnerability of the Skin," in *The Face of the Other and the Trace of God*, ed. Jeffrey Bloechl (New York: Fordham University Press, 2000), 45-46.

28. Levinas, *Otherwise than Being*, 14.

29. Gilles Deleuze, *Francis Bacon: The Logic of Sensation*, trans. Daniel W. Smith (Minneapolis: University of Minnesota Press, 2003), 36.

30. For Heidegger, Dasein is always ecstatically outside itself insofar as it is fundamentally a temporal being. Among the three "ecstases" of time, the future is the most primordial for Dasein. Dasein is a future-directed being, engaged in projects, for itself, and always being towards its own death. The same is true for Merleau-Ponty's subject of perception. If temporality is a basic ontological structure of Dasein's being for Heidegger, then affectivity is such for Levinas. On temporality, see Martin Heidegger, *Being and Time*, John Macquarrie and Edward Robinson (San Francisco: HarperCollins, 1962), 377-378ff.

31. Emmanuel Levinas, *Totality and Infinity*, trans. Alphonso Lingis (Pittsburgh: Duquesne University Press, 1969), 111.

32. Levinas, *Totality and Infinity*, 114.

33. Levinas, *Totality and Infinity*, 111.

34. Silvia Benso, "The Breathing of the Air: Presocratic Echoes in Levinas," in *Levinas and the Ancients*, eds. Brian Schroeder and Silvia Benso (Bloomington: Indiana University Press, 2008), 20.

35. Hans Jonas, *The Phenomenon of Life* (Evanston: Northwestern University Press, 1966), 71, fn.13. The concept of metabolism need not be confined to philosophical biology, but can be

deployed generally as a description of the genesis of form out of any material interaction. On the immanent genesis of form, see Manuel DeLanda, "Immanence and Transcendence in the Genesis of Form," *The South Atlantic Quarterly* 96, no. 3 (Summer 1997): 499-514.

36. See, for example, Levinas, *Totality and Infinity*, 118; *Otherwise than Being*, 73; and Emmanuel Levinas, *Existence and Existents*, trans. Alphonso Lingis (Pittsburgh: Duquesne University Press, 1988), 81.

37. Levinas, *Totality and Infinity*, 115.

38. Incidentally, Merleau-Ponty calls affective life "the birth of being for us," in *Phenomenology of Perception*, 154.

39. Levinas, *Phenomenology of Perception*, 209.

40. Levinas, *Phenomenology of Perception*, 211. On the body as power, see also *Phenomenology*, 142, 143, 210, 302. It should be noted that Merleau-Ponty specifies that the body is synchronized with the *existential* world, not the *sensible*, which remains at all times foreign and disruptive of the body's competence. That is, there is a basic diachrony or dissymmetry between the subject of perception and the sensible environment.

41. The "flesh" names the impersonal, anonymous form of the sensible in general. It is what unites both seer and seen; or, more precisely, it is the visible as such. Merleau-Ponty calls the flesh the common "element" that subjects and objects emerge from, indicating that "the thickness of flesh between seer and the thing is constitutive for the thing of its visibility as for the seer of his corporeity." See Maurice Merleau-Ponty, *The Visible and the Invisible*, trans. Alphonso Lingis (Evanston: Northwestern University Press, 1968), 135.

42. Merleau-Ponty, *Phenomenology of Perception*, 302.

43. Alphonso Lingis, *Foreign Bodies* (New York: Routledge, 1994), 15.

44. Merleau-Ponty, *Phenomenology*, 140. Lingis takes sides with

Levinas against Merleau-Ponty when he writes in *Foreign Bodies*, 24-25: "In the substance of our competence other bodies emerge, ethereal and phantasmal—bodies that materialize forces and powers that are other than those of praktognostic competence."

45. Merleau-Ponty, *Phenomenology of Perception*, 137.

46. Merleau-Ponty, *Phenomenology of Perception*, 249. Conceiving the body as a mosaic can be useful for thinking about the constitution of racial identities. This work is being done, although not from a phenomenological perspective, by historian Mark M. Smith. See *How Race is Made: Slavery, Segregation, and the Senses* (Chapel Hill: University of North Carolina Press, 2006).

47. George Berkeley, *A Treatise Concerning the Principles of Human Knowledge* (Indianapolis: Hackett, 1982), Part I, §1.

48. Merleau-Ponty, *Phenomenology of Perception*, 215.

49. Gilles Deleuze, *Empiricism and Subjectivity*, trans. Constantin V. Boundas (New York: Columbia University Press, 1991), 23, emphasis added. Deleuze is commenting on the personal identity section of Hume's *Treatise*.

50. William James, *Psychology: The Briefer Course* (Mineola, NY: Dover, 2001), 2. Catherine Malabou draws an important distinction between plasticity and flexibility when she says that, "To be flexible is to receive a form or impression, to be able to fold oneself, to take the fold, not to give it. To be docile, to not explode. Indeed, what flexibility lacks is the resource of giving form, the power to create, to invent or even to erase an impression, the power to style. Flexibility is plasticity minus its genius." See her *What Should We Do with Our Brain?*, trans. Sebastian Rand (New York: Fordham University Press, 2008), 12. The creative aspect of plasticity is central to the concept, even though I have downplayed that aspect here.

51. Merleau-Ponty, *Phenomenology of Perception*, 150: "The body is

to be compared, not to a physical object, but rather to a work of art."

52. Merleau-Ponty, *Phenomenology of Perception*, 302.

53. Merleau-Ponty, *Phenomenology of Perception*, 302.

54. Maurice Merleau-Ponty, "Cézanne's Doubt," in *Sense and Non-Sense*, trans. Hubert L. Dreyfus and Patricia Allen Dreyfus (Evanston: Northwestern University Press, 1964), 15.

55. Questions regarding the prosthetic, machinic, and non-organic nature of the body arise at this point.

56. I am thinking here of what Erich Schiffman calls the "edge" of a yoga posture (*asana*). An edge is defined by the *intensity* of the posture, the point at which the body is stretched to the verge of pain, but at the same time increasing its physical potential. "Edges," writes Schiffmann, "are marked by pain and define your limits." Without this degree of pain, "there is no challenge to the muscles, no intensity, no stretch, and little possibility for opening. Going too far, however, is an obvious violation of the body, increasing the possibility of both physical pain and injury." See *Yoga: The Spirit and Practice of Moving into Stillness* (New York: Pocket Books, 1996), 74.

57. Edward S. Casey, *Getting Back into Place* (Bloomington: Indiana University Press, 1993), 292.

58. Casey, *Getting Back into Place*, 293. See also Merleau-Ponty, *Phenomenology of Perception*, 142-143, on the cultivation of habit as the acquisition of power. For full treatment of the concept of *habitus*, see Pierre Bourdieu, *The Logic of Practice*, trans. Richard Nice (Stanford: Stanford University Press, 1992).

59. Malabou, *What Should We Do with Our Brain?*, 12. Gail Weiss criticizes Boudieu's concept of *habitus* for being too deterministic, for not allowing enough room for individual freedom or self-stylization of the *habitus*. Bourdieu, then, has

"difficulty explaining how radical change or spontaneous innovation can really occur either on an individual or on a societal level." She tries to overcomes Bourdieu's defects by supplementing his thinking with the insights of phenomenologists like Merleau-Ponty. See *Refiguring the Ordinary* (Bloomington: Indiana University Press, 2008), 86-87. I remain skeptical about the reality of radical change, and therefore sympathize with Bourdieu's quasi-deterministic characterization of the *habitus*.

60. I want to suggest that notions like "atmosphere," "aura," and "ambience" can be accounted for in terms of sensation. In a sense, then, to say that something possesses an atmosphere, without specifying the elements of that atmosphere, is a failure of description. Ideally a unique atmosphere should be specifiable in terms of the singular set of sensations it gives off—its sensory signature or fingerprint, so to speak.

61. Peter Zumthor, *Atmospheres* (Basel: Birkhäuser, 2006), 23.

62. See Juhani Pallasmaa, "An Architecture of the Seven Senses," in Steven Holl et al., *Questions of Perception* (San Francisco: William Stout, 2008), 36-37. Pallasmaa sees the skin as central to this process. He explores this further in *The Eyes of the Skin: Architecture and the Senses*, second edition (Academy Press, 2005).

63. Pallasmaa, "An Architecture of the Seven Senses," 41.

64. This ethical sentiment is highlighted in Frank Lloyd Wright's writing on the natural home, where his conception of architectural integrity is motivated by a balanced concern for the natural and built environments. This means above all that his design pays particular attention to the *interface* of site and building, and tries to preserve the integrity of both while at the same time introducing a new aesthetic dimension. As a result, the building site is intensified, not degraded or diluted. See Wright's essay, "Integrity," in *The Natural House* (New York: Bramhall House, 1954).

65. The "Sounds" chapter of *Walden* illustrates the aural identity of the book's namesake. The birdsongs, train whistles, cars, bells, etc. that Thoreau records are what get coded as "Walden." From the standpoint of the ear, Walden just is this aggregate of sounds. See Henry David Thoreau, *Walden and Other Writings* (New York: Bantam, 1983).

66. Gong Szeto, "Towards a General Theory of Value: An Interview with Michael Benedikt." March 6, 2003. *American Institute of Graphic Arts*, http://gain2.aiga.org/content .cfm?Alias=michaelbenedikt&rca=michaelbenedikt1&pff=1

67. In addition to *What Should We Do with Our Brain?*, see Malabou's *The Future of Hegel: Plasticity, Temporality, and Dialectic*, trans. Lisabeth During (London: Routledge, 2004), *Plasticity at the Dusk of Writing: Dialectic, Destruction, Deconstruction*, trans. Carolyn Shread (New York: Columbia University Press, 2009), and *Ontology of the Accident: An Essay on Destructive Plasticity*, trans. Carolyn Shread (Cambridge: Polity, 2012).

68. Elizabeth Grosz, "Lived Spatiality," in *Architecture from the Outside: Essays on Virtual and Real Space* (Cambridge, MA: MIT Press, 2001), 32.

69. See the "brief preface concerning the nature of bodies" in Part II (pp. 72-76) of Baruch Spinoza, *Ethics*, trans. Samuel Shirley (Indianapolis: Hackett, 1992).

70 Gilles Deleuze, *Nietzsche and Philosophy*, trans. Hugh Tomlinson (New York: Columbia University Press, 1983), 17.

71. James C. Morrison, "Why Spinoza Had No Aesthetics," *Journal of Aesthetics and Art Criticism* 47, no. 4 (Fall 1989): 359-365, argues that Spinoza had no aesthetics, and for good reason. If we take aesthetics in the expanded sense that I have advocated in this essay, rather than in the narrow sense of "philosophy of art and beauty" employed by Morrison, then Spinoza has much to offer us.

72. See, for instance, Eccy de Jonge, *Spinoza and Deep Ecology*

(Burlington: Ashgate, 2004) and Gilles Deleuze, *Spinoza: Practical Philosophy*, trans. Robert Hurley (San Francisco: City Lights, 1988).

73. On this point, see Timothy Morton's *The Ecological Thought* (Cambridge, MA: Harvard University Press, 2010).

4

Strange Ecology

Introduction

There is currently a lot of interest in how Levinas's philosophy can be used to work out some problems in environmental philosophy and environmental ethics. One strategy, which has come under recent criticism, attempts to take Levinas's concept of "the face" (*le visage*) and impart its ethical significance to nonhuman animals or the natural environment. This strategy can only succeed if the face is indeed something that can be exported from the human world and imported into the nonhuman world. There are, however, a number of compelling reasons to be skeptical about the possibility of transferring the face from the human to the nonhuman, and I discuss these in the first part of this chapter. In the second part I argue that, despite the properly human character of the face, the otherness it harbors provides us with a clue to the irreducible and startling strangeness of ecological life. To draw out this point I lean on Timothy Morton's *The Ecological Thought*, particularly his concept of "dark ecology." What I conclude is that Levinas's ethics has little to teach us about environmental ethics, but much to teach us about the meaning of ecology as well as what it might take to supply an ethics which responds to the wonderfully strange and shadowy network of others populating our ecosystems.

The Face of Nature?

As is well known, Levinas chooses "the face" as the figure meant to signify just how the (human) Other arrives on the scene to solicit me for help. Otherwise engrossed in the everyday struggle for self-preservation, the self, when faced by the Other, finds itself interrupted and obliged to accommodate the needs of the

Other—whatever these needs may be. In this respect the solicitation of the Other which comes via the face imposes an excessive
obligation on the self. The excessive nature of this obligation
derives from the fact that "the Other remains infinitely
transcendent, infinitely foreign; his face in which his epiphany is
produced and which appeals to me breaks with the world that
can be common to us, whose virtualities are inscribed in our
nature and developed by our existence" (TI 194).[1] The ethical
force of the Other's face resides in its "total resistance" to my
power, the way in which the face—otherwise called by Levinas
the "idea of infinity" (TI 51)—eludes my power to murder and
thereby establishes "a relation not with a very great resistance,
but with something absolutely *other*: the resistance of what has no
resistance—the ethical resistance" (TI 199). The face-to-face
encounter, in short, is the site of an ethical command that
empowers me to respond at the same time as it exceeds my
capacity to respond adequately.

The worry for environmental ethicists wondering about how
Levinas can help their cause is over the question of whether or
not the face is a strictly anthropocentric concept. If it is, then it
would be inappropriate to attribute an ethical significance to the
face of animals or the face of a wetland, for example. The
language that Levinas consistently employs to characterize the
ethical force of the face suggests not only humanity, but divinity.
It would seem that the face is always the face of a human being
or the face of God. Passages like the following are typical: "The
nakedness of the face is destituteness. To recognize the Other is
to recognize a hunger. To recognize the Other is to give. But it is
to give to the master, to the lord, to him whom one approaches as
"You" in a dimension of height" (TI 75). The animal and the
wetland do not speak a supplication from this dimension of
height because, on the one hand, they do not speak at all and, on
the other, it is not clear where one would look into the face of a
wetland or, odd as it may sound, an animal. Understanding what

it means to say that an animal lacks a face is critical to understanding ethics as Levinas conceives it.

Christian Diehm identifies two problems with transferring the concept of the face to nonhumans.[2] The first we can call the "experiential problem." Insofar as the face is supposed to reveal my responsibility to me phenomenologically and bear a concrete or even visible dimension, it is not clear how one could experience certain ecological phenomena like ecosystems or species, let alone the imperatives they command. The vastness and/or abstractness of these realities entails that they cannot be given phenomenologically. This is, I think, only a problem if we insist that Levinas's ethics is fundamentally phenomenological. The second problem for a non-anthropocentric Levinasian ethics we will call the "alterity problem." Diehm points out that, for Levinas, "ethical experience entails having the legitimacy of our own projects called into question in light of the projects of others; it is to find ourselves concerned about the ways in which others can be denied what they need or have the pursuit of their goods take a turn for the worse."[3] Even if an ecosystem or a wetland has concrete aspects which are describable phenomenologically, the fact that they are not beings-for-themselves would mean that they do not possess the alterity proper to those entities—namely, humans—that contest the justice of our projects with their own needs. But even if we admit that nonhuman entities possess the kind of project-oriented alterity that would call into question the morality of our human endeavors, I do not think that this quite captures the dimension of height or divinity that Levinas explicitly attributes to the Other. This is a general hesitation that I have about what can count as *wholly other* (other in the capitalized, superlative sense—Other) for Levinas.

The more specific hesitation I have concerns where we might encounter the face of the environment. Given that Levinas famously wavered on the question of whether or not animals have faces, and at times admitted that "the priority...is not found in the animal, but in the human face,"[4] there is good reason to be suspicious about the existence of a face of the environment. Peter Atterton, however, proposes that it is possible to extend moral considerability to the environment using Levinasian principles. He does not directly suggest that Levinasian ethics speaks to environmental ethics, although it is instructive to see why he believes the face is applicable to, at the least, animals.[5] Atterton reminds us first that Levinas does not insist on a *conceptual* link between the face and the human species. While it is true that only beings with a "face" qualify as "Other"—with all of the ethical baggage entailed therein—it is not necessary that the Other be human, but rather that this other be capable of *experiencing a need* and articulating a moral claim on me, a claim that singles me out as someone responsible for relieving the Other's need.[6] The expression of needs does not require language for its articulation, but is something that can be read even in the eyes or the nape of the Other. Anywhere that suffering or indigence is readable, there we may find the face of the Other commanding responsibility and soliciting our conscience. But what does this moral literacy entail? The problem with interpreting the ethical command of the face in Atterton's terms—as witnessing and responding to suffering wherever it's legible—is that it leaves open the question, *Whence the source of the ethical command?* In other words, if it is maintained that the ethical force of the face transcends any concrete particular, and that the face is more than the physiognomy of a suffering creature, then phenomenologically speaking it becomes difficult (if not impossible) to tell if animal suffering and human suffering express equally the ethical imperative.[7] Even if the concept of the face entails properties like sentience, or the capacity to feel pleasure and pain, it is not enough to say that the face commands wherever suffering is expressed and my conscience is aroused by that suffering. Such a view would not only preclude us from using Levinasian ethics to address a whole set of environmental problems that have nothing to do with sentient suffering, it also seems to miss Levinas's fundamental point: that the face of the Other empowers me to respond to suffering *prior to* any particular expression of suffering. The transcendental dimension of Levinas's thought gets lost when his ethics is read too closely with utilitarian, or even phenomenological, philosophy. The empowerment generated in the self by the Other is not merely the capacity relieve suffering, but the imperative that we *must* assume responsibility for suffering no matter what. This imperative, as Diane Perpich has argued, binds our "responsibility for the other *because of the other* or *for the sake of the other* in his or her irreducible alterity and singularity."[8] The singularity of the Other or her singular expression of need does not cause the ethical imperative to relieve needfulness or suffering—this is not Levinas's point—but instead demands that I justify this suffering to those faces who suffer and who solicit my help.[9]

Do dogs, snakes, trees, mountains, or rivers demand that we humans justify our actions? In other words, do these nonhuman entities have faces? In many ways this question seems misguided; it seems too anthropocentric to be any good for environmental philosophy. In another respect, it's simply not something Levinas asks. He never troubles himself with the environment, and there is good reason to believe that searching for the environmental equivalent of the face will always lead us back to the admittedly featureless (because formless, immaterial) face of the Other, which is nevertheless the face of the human. When Levinas deploys the face, it is always to invoke the idea of God, the idea of infinity and an infinite responsibility.

Levinas's neglect of environmental issues and his anthropocentric account of responsibility should not dissuade us from recognizing his relevance for ecological thinking. His concept of the face points us, indeed, to a deep truth about what I will refer to as "ecological life," by which I mean what it is like to live amid a network of interdependent beings, the vast majority of which are unknown and, in a real sense, unknowable to us.

Strange Others

What I find so alluring about Levinas's philosophy is the profound sense of strangeness that pervades so many of his discussions. Indeed, I might even say that his philosophy can only get off the ground if one is capable of grasping the utter weirdness of his thinking about intersubjectivity, difference, alterity, and ethics. It is worth noting that much of the strangeness is concentrated in the face of the Other and it is in the face that we are asked to confront just how foreign—and how dark—our world truly is.

In a discussion of discourse and language in *Totality and Infinity* (73), Levinas finds himself exclaiming the foreignness of the Other's freedom in order to emphasize the strangeness of this freedom. These descriptions are typical of Levinas. Discourse, he says, is the very experience of "something absolutely foreign" to me; it is a "traumatism of astonishment." "Free beings alone can be strangers to one another." Language itself presupposes this strangeness and is precisely a means of mediating strangeness with a common currency. When Levinas speaks of the face he often stresses its liminal nature, the way in which it straddles the perceptible and imperceptible realms, the worlds of matter and spirit. The face is a genuine incarnation in the Judeo-Christian sense. It is at once immanent and transcendent, intelligible and unintelligible, visible in light and shrouded in darkness. It paradoxically expresses the inexpressible, which is why Levinas calls it an enigma. This is the Other's "condition of being a stranger" (TI 75). Language, perception, and thought allow us to grasp the strangeness of the Other, but they ultimately leave us incapable of adequately understanding this entity that Timothy Morton calls the *strange stranger*.

The face of the Other, then, is essentially the site of an excessive strangeness. But it is its paradoxical and enigmatic nature, rather than its transcendence, I contend, that renders it strange. The face expresses what Levinas refers to as infinity, and it is this infinity—this radical otherness—that disarms me with its "absolute resistance" of my capacity to comprehend, violate, or murder it.[10] Confronting the face of the Other is like attempting to think infinity with a finite intellect. Although infinity can be rendered intelligible, your ability to conceive infinity is surpassed by the radical alterity of infinity. (Again, read Descartes.) The finite cannot contain the infinite; infinity overflows the thought that thinks it. As Levinas says, "in thinking infinity the I from the first *thinks more than it thinks*."[11] The Other, as transcendent, is infinitely separated from me, and thus is never fully present to my gaze or my intellect. Nevertheless, the Other is capable of presenting herself to me as something that conditions my freedom and my power.[12] Otherwise put, the Other is present in me as the source of my freedom to respond to the Other's needs. Without the other I am powerless: without recourse, without resources, and incapable of response. This "apparition," this "undesirable stranger," is the ground of ethical resistance—and, like it or not, is intimately connected to me, vulnerable and dependent on me.[13]

When I realize that my freedom, action, and responsibility are intimately connected to the freedom and vulnerability of countless other humans and nonhumans, and that these others not only exceed my ability to cognize their plurality, but even exceed my capacity to grasp their singularity, I realize that I am caught up in what Morton calls "the mesh." The mesh is another name for the system of coexistence and codependence that marks life on Earth. The mesh refers us to how, when we try to conceive the vastness of ecological life—and the way in which everything whatsoever is connected to everything else—we discern that there is neither center nor edge of the environment. The environment is, paradoxically, *absolutely everywhere and nowhere as the same time.*[14] As Morton puts it:

Thinking interdependence involves dissolving the barrier between "over here" and "over there," and more fundamentally, the metaphysical illusion of rigid, narrow boundaries between inside and outside. Thinking interdependence involves thinking difference. This means confronting the fact that all beings are related to each other negatively and differentially, in an open system without center or edge.[15]

When we actually attempt to think the system of radical interdependence we find ourselves caught up in, we are forced to think what Morton calls "the ecological thought." The ecological thought requires us to try to imagine all the beings that make up our ecosystems as well as the links between every one of these ecosystems, or the totality of strange strangers. A strange stranger is a being—human, animal, other—that is simultaneously intimate with and foreign to me. The more you look at and learn about this intimacy, the more foreign the strange stranger seems. This is the nature of its strangeness and the effect it has on our thinking.[16] The strange stranger is not just some exotic species of insect or weed that lives on the far side of the planet, vulnerable to anthropogenic climate change: it is your closest neighbor or housecat or long-term partner. "The more we know them, the stranger they become." Their strangeness derives precisely from the fact that we can never anticipate or know them, from the way their familiarity becomes so familiar it becomes quite unfamiliar, like a word you say over and over and over and over again until you are convinced that you are not pronouncing it properly. It sounds so weird all of a sudden! This is the strangeness of infinity, which demonstrates just how intimacy serves to intensify foreignness.[17] It is particularly disarming to acknowledge that it is precisely this strangeness that commands us ethically, that calls for our humility and caution. The strange stranger is the face(lessness) of infinity, the specter of a responsibility that exceeds us.

Facelessness

To think the ecological thought it is not enough to encounter the strange stranger face-to-face and be struck with the weirdness of its intimacy. And it is not enough to imagine the immense network of things that make up ecological life. The ecological thought requires us to recognize that there is no adequate perspective on the environment that would enable us to look it in the face. The environment faces us from every angle; it is every-where we look and everywhere we don't. It both surrounds us and inhabits us and in the final analysis this means that we have no inside or outside, and thus we ourselves are nothing other than one of the strange strangers that haunt us. And if it is true that climate change, for example, or any of the other "hyperob-jects" identified by Morton, presents us with an environmental crisis that requires ethical and political responses, then we have good reason to be terrified at how the ecological thought resists our capacity to think it at the same time as it commands us to think it.

When we try to imagine the threat to ecological life posed by the climate crisis, we are met with the kind of horror that Levinas attributes to the *il y a*, bare existence, or the night in its purest darkness. This is because, while science shows that humanity does in fact play a role in climate change, we are not really in a position to respond to the solicitation of climate in the way we may respond to the question, "May I have a drink of water?" Climate does not speak, nor does it ask us to justify our actions, of course, but this is also not the point. The real problem is that climate—or the environment more generally—*holds us hostage* at the same time as it asks for our help. The environment is not some object that stands out for us against a background or horizon, and if it "speaks" to us it is with a disembodied voice that one might encounter only in a play by Beckett. The environment is the background, foreground, and object all collapsed into one; it is what Levinas calls a nothing that is not a pure nothingness.[18] The environment, like the there is (*il y a*), "is no longer *this* or *that*; there is not 'something'" called environment or climate.[19] The environment, like the night in Levinas, is the dissolution of form and a depersonalizing agent that is the very dissolution of perspective.[20] Husserl famously says somewhere that even God could not achieve a perspectiveless view on an object. This is a phenomenological fact, but one that is dissolved by the environment. The environment achieves what even God cannot. It makes contact with everything without approaching anything from a particular angle of view. It is an anonymous something, yet it is the most intimate phenomenon, offering us no escape and no clear means of dealing with its challenges. We know that something must be done about climate change, but this something is frighteningly indeterminate. The horror of ecological life is its ubiquitous facelessness and the urgency of its imperative.

At best the environment as such is the strangest of strangers. When we confront environmental crises we know that "something is happening,"[21] but it is so difficult to know how to respond because the environment solicits us from every possible angle like a presence that is felt but never identified. "It's as if there is something else—someone else, even—but the more we look, the less sure we are. It's uncanny: there is something there, and there isn't."[22] Such is the horror of ecological life, and such is the exigency of environmental ethics.

Notes

1. Emmanuel Levinas, *Totality and Infinity*, trans. Alphonso Lingis (Pittsburgh: Duquesne University Press, 1969). All references to this text cited parenthetically as TI.

2. Christian Diehm, "Alterity, Value, Autonomy: Levinas and Environmental Ethics," in *Facing Nature: Levinas and Environmental Thought*, eds. William Edelglass, James Hatley, and Christian Diehm (Pittsburgh: Duquesne University

Press, 2012), 19.

3. Diehm, "Alterity, Value, Autonomy," 19.

4. Emmanuel Levinas, "The Paradox of Morality: An Interview with Emmanuel Levinas," quoted in Peter Atterton, "Facing Animals," in *Facing Nature*, 33.

5. Atterton, "Facing Animals," 25.

6. Atterton, "Facing Animals," 27-28.

7. Atterton, "Facing Animals," 36.

8. Diane Perpich, "Scarce Resources? Levinas, Animals, and the Environment," in *Facing Nature*, 78.

9. Perpich, "Scarce Resources," 93.

10. Emmanuel Levinas, "Philosophy and the Idea of Infinity," in *Collected Philosophical Papers*, trans. Alphonso Lingis (Pittsburgh: Duquesne University Press, 1987), 54.

11. Levinas, "Philosophy and the Idea of Infinity," 54.

12. Levinas, "Philosophy and the Idea of Infinity," 55.

13. Levinas, "Phenomenon and Enigma," in *Collected Philosophical Papers*, 70.

14. Timothy Morton, *The Ecological Thought* (Cambridge, MA: Harvard University Press, 2010), 29.

15. Morton, *The Ecological Thought*, 39.

16. Morton, *The Ecological Thought*, 41.

17. Morton, *The Ecological Thought*, 42.

18. Morton, *The Ecological Thought*, 28, 88.

19. Emmanuel Levinas, *Existence and Existents*, trans. Alphonso Lingis (Pittsburgh: Duquesne University Press, 1988), 52.

20. Levinas, *Existence and Existents*, 53.

21. Levinas, *Existence and Existents*, 52.

22. Morton, *The Ecological Thought*, 53.

5

Complexions

Introduction

Levinas is a philosopher of startling sincerity. But despite his earnestness and appeal among continental philosophers, the theological dimension of his thinking and rhetoric causes many would-be sympathizers to shy away from him. The notion that "the face of the Other" gains its ultimate significance by revealing the presence of divinity is seen as needless hyperbole. I think Levinas need not be so radical in his account of the face, that his ethics could retain its force even if it abandoned its theological foundation for a secular one. Such a feat impels the work of Alphonso Lingis, and the following chapter shows at length how this is done.

The present chapter offers a critical analysis of Levinas's conception of the face *as revelation* and suggests a reappraisal of the face-to-face encounter that is informed by Levinas's analysis of sensibility. One could see it as providing a phenomenological, or perhaps realist, reading of the face that substitutes for Levinas's "metaphysical" reading. Focusing on the materiality of the ethical relation, it adduces some of the dangers of his construal of the face and explores an alternative interpretation of faciality; this interpretation is not a departure from Levinas, but rather a defense of what Robert Bernasconi has called the "empiricist" reading.[1] By refocusing his project on the sensuous aspects of faciality, Levinas is better prepared to confront criticism from potential detractors in feminist and critical race theory, or other fields that emphasize the corporeality of relations. For this, it must be shown that the material complexity of the Other is what places him/her beyond *comprehension*, without putting them beyond *contact*. A mundane ethical contact which forgets about divine commandments can be assembled from Levinas's own tools, thus displacing from his obsession with transcendence. This requires thinking the face as immanent infinity, or as a sensuously textured presence that gestures toward countless faces in their stark mortality.

Totalities

Totality and Infinity is a work driven by its critique of systematic ontology, Hegel and Heidegger in particular, both of whom stand as representatives of what Levinas terms "totality." Totality is shorthand for any closed system which leaves no room for radical alterity. Idealist philosophies, with their reductive conceptual schemata and all-inclusive representations, are a favorite target for Levinas. The Hegelian totality, for instance, considers the world as the manifestation of an organic human spirit incapable of seeing the world as irrational or beyond cognition, that is, as other. What Levinas finds objectionable about Hegel, as well as Heidegger, is that they build ontological systems that reduce or exclude otherness and difference in the name of universal sameness. Levinas opposes totalizing systems with the concept of infinity, which is emblematic of that which cannot be enclosed within a system because its very being is constituted by its excess. Think Descartes's idea of God in the Third Meditation. Infinity is what overflows the finitude of any system; infinity is that which resists inclusion. The most prominent instantiation of infinity, at least in *Totality and Infinity* and several other important essays, appears in the revelation of "the face" (*le visage*). Levinas does not mean the fleshy, tangible face that we encounter when we look at another person. Nor is the face a simple metaphor, although it is a metaphor. The face for Levinas is much more: the face is (and is not) the face of God, a divine and disincarnate presence which speaks, but *does not appear*, through the eyes of another person.[2] The elevation of the face to such a height can be difficult to accept, but it is constitutive of the very force of Levinasian philosophy. To understand the ethical function of the face, it is necessary to see how it interrupts—as infinity and transcendence—and precedes an ontology like Heidegger's.

The exigency of infinity in Levinas's ethics is fuelled by the tendency of Western philosophy to place ontology before ethics. Ethics is always made to conform itself to the guidelines of ontology, which inevitably seeks to comprehend individual beings within a general system of being. By forcing every being to conform to a single system, ontology necessarily does violence to whatever resists enclosure, whether by referring its singularity to a general form or by excluding it as nonsensical. Ontological closure needs to be overcome, according to Levinas, by installing ethics as first philosophy, thus guaranteeing a minimization of violence in our philosophical systems and political institutions.[3] Putting ethics before ontology means ensuring that difference is not effaced by the normative standards of life in common or the world of the same. Ontology must conform to ethics, not the other way around.

The philosophy of intersubjectivity, when guided by ontology instead of ethics, runs the risk of building a world that is intolerant of alterity, which allows no place for the Other as other. Even, and especially, Heideggerian ontology enacts a violent exclusion of this kind. Heidegger's philosophy, and by implication his politics, institutes a "pagan climate" that Levinas considers intolerable and genuinely dangerous.[4] Being is the oppressive specter of Heidegger's system—its oppression is precisely its neutral universal gaze, which remains blind to the infinite distance which separates my subjectivity from others. In his interrogation of being, according to Levinas, Heidegger fails to comprehend the elevation of the Other at the same time that he succeeds in assimilating the transcendence of the Other into the immanent structure of being-in-the-world.[5] Levinas cites the basic structure of Dasein (as care, *Sorge*) and the exposition of

Mitsein (being-with) in *Being and Time* to illustrate the ethical neutrality of Heideggerian ontology: both of these structures refer intersubjectivity to the immanent structures of ontology, and therefore remain silent about what lies beyond being. "In Heidegger coexistence is, to be sure, taken as a relationship with the Other irreducible to objective cognition; but in the final analysis it also rests on the relationship with *being in general*, on comprehension, on ontology."[6] Before *Sorge* and *Mitsein*, the ethical relation structures the world-in-common and makes it inhabitable; it is the Good, beyond being, which nourishes our concernful being-with. This is Levinas's claim.

Levinas calls the face-to-face *the* ethical relation because it is the site where the Other calls the autonomous ego to account for itself, to be accountable for its freedom and its personal projections. The Other does not properly appear as an object for the ego, but nevertheless contests the field of visibility which the ego projects by claiming that field of visibility as its own. A struggle ensues. But the contestation brought upon the ego by the Other is itself incontestable because the ego contested remains ignorant of who is contesting it. Or, as Marion says,

> I do not accede to the other by seeing more, better, or otherwise, but by renouncing mastery over the visible so as to see objects within it, and thus by letting myself be glimpsed by a gaze which sees me without my seeing it—a gaze which, invisibly and beyond my aims, silently swallows me up and submerges me, whether I know it or not, whether or not I want it to do so.[7]

The ethicality of the face-to-face encounter derives from its asymmetrical structure, or the fact that an ego is unable to comprehend the Other beyond the objective presence which appears to it as that which remains concealed. As in Descartes, it bears the structure of a finite intellect coming into contact with the idea of God: an infinite depth is found in the face of the Other.[8] The encounter with the infinite renders the finite ego passive. Passivity is the only mode possible for a finite intellect prompted to accommodate an infinite power, and the condition of possibility for responsibility.[9] Because they lack this asymmetrical dimension, Heidegger's neutral ontology of being-with and Buber's symmetrical I-Thou dialogue, for example, do not qualify the intersubjective relation as immediately ethical.[10]

In Heidegger, being-with is always comprehended against the horizon of equipmentality, of the *Zuhandenheit* he sees as primary to Dasein's understanding of its being-in-the-world.[11] Since the Other always appears within a system of pre-understood referentiality, the Other is able to communicate and interact with me. The equipmental horizon is basic to the ontological structure of Dasein: all of Dasein's relations must pass through this tool-system, and thus through being. For Levinas, the obligatory passage through being which Heidegger forces every existent to undergo is the neutralization of otherness, the necessary reduction of the truth of the Other to a system of established references. Hannah Arendt describes Heidegger's system of equipment in the following terms:

> [T]here exists a web of human relationships which is, as it were, woven by deeds and words of innumerable persons, by the living as well as by the dead. Every deed and every new beginning falls into an already existing web where it nevertheless somehow starts a new process that will affect many others even beyond those with whom the agent comes into direct contact.[12]

That every deed triggers a new series of effects is what makes Levinas eager to formulate an adequate theory of justice. The unforeseeable effects which issue from Dasein's freedom and the analysis of intersubjectivity are never called before an ethical tribunal, precisely because Heidegger's conception of *Mitsein* remains at the level of a universal law. For Levinas, its anonymity is precisely its inadequacy: "Universality presents itself as impersonal; and this is another inhumanity."[13] This means that the freedom of Dasein is never really held responsible for its actions, because its actions never run up against a vulnerable and affected Other, which is the vehicle of justice in Levinas's metaphysics.[14]

To counteract Heidegger's inhumanity without completely dismissing his ontology, Levinas puts the face of existents before being, thus reversing the Heideggerian model. Levinas needs the face to condition, or "signify beyond," the meaning of any hermeneutic or phenomenological horizon.[15] Not included in this horizon, however and this is representative of everything that is insufficient in Heidegger's account of being-in-the-world and being-with-others—are the concrete needs of human beings, which Heidegger brackets from his ontological considerations as merely "ontic" concerns. As Levinas says in *Totality and Infinity*, "Dasein is never hungry." With this pithy remark, Levinas means to charge Heidegger with a decisive unconcern for everyday human needs. This is Heidegger's fatal flaw. But is it not also Levinas's? Does he not, somewhat tragically, commit the same error in his metaphysics of the face despite the extensive attention he gives to needfulness in his first magnum opus? That is to say, is it not the case that the face of the Other which summons my responsibility is superseded by the more-than-human face of God, thereby destroying the singular humanity of the Other's imperative?

Elevation and Recognition

Levinas believes he can grant ethical significance to the face only by elevating it to a level beyond any representational system of knowledge. This means that the face cannot be allowed to *appear*; it may only *signify*. Or, as Edith Wyschogrod puts it, "the face breaks with the sensible form which appears to contain it by addressing us, by soliciting a relationship with it which cannot be expressed in terms of enjoyment or knowledge."[16] Levinas must therefore give the face a metaphysical, as opposed to ontological, meaning. Ontology, in Levinas's terms, confines us to immanence, whereas metaphysics refers our gaze beyond the face of the Other, to the realm of transcendence, which is precisely where the singularity of the Other resides. The singularity of the Other is shut away behind the eyes, at an infinite remove from any representation the ego could construct. The metaphysical elevation of the face allows Levinas to avoid the inevitably agonistic forms of intersubjectivity that arise in symmetrical models, such as those found in rationalistic discourse ethics, Hegel's master-slave dialectic, or even Buber's dialogism. By rendering the ethical relation asymmetrical, Levinas can argue that all war or agonism presupposes peaceful solicitations, and therefore every encounter is derivative of a peace that I am obligated to maintain.[17] I must always assume, or rather admit, that the Other approaches me peacefully. Ethics becomes for Levinas an ideal metaphysical communion, a nonviolent relation where two transcendences meet without touching. Ethics bridges the chasm across which the Other obligates me to respond and constitutes the otherwise neutral realm of intersubjectivity.

I reject the distinction which Levinas draws between ontology and metaphysics, but I only want to say in defense that by making the face a transcendental condition of subjectivity, Levinas gives an ontological meaning to it, if by "ontology" we mean the question of what is, as it is. Calling his ethical project "metaphysics" seems to put certain questions out of play and to distance Levinas from the history of metaphysics traditionally conceived, thereby weakening the power of his argument, which seems to demand an uncritical reception. In short, if Levinas wants to redefine "metaphysics," he may, but this seems to involve a private language that fails to communicate with other metaphysicians. This failure of communication is not a foregone conclusion, however. I think he has much to teach metaphysics as it is usually understood.

Levinas's account of the face strips the face of its phenomenality, and therefore renders the face unrecognizable in its singularity. This is problematic. It compromises the ability of the face to appear to us within immanence, and therefore divests the face of its phenomenologically evident imperative. Just as Heidegger's Dasein is never hungry, Levinas's face never laughs or cries; its eyes do not shimmer before our own. As he emphatically puts it in *Ethics and Infinity*, "The best way of encountering the Other is not even to notice the color of his eyes!"[18] Or, in *Totality and Infinity*: "The eye does not shine; it speaks."[19] Marion is reading Levinas correctly when he writes that to face the Other is to concentrate one's gaze on the pupil of the eye, the precise vanishing point of the Other: "here, for the first time, in the very midst of the visible, there is nothing to see, except an invisible and untargetable void."[20]

The eyes modestly conceal the Other who faces, but they at the same time reveal an abstract system of subjection which contains both enabling and disabling components.[21] The eyes are essential to the functioning of this system, acting as both window (onto the unknown) and mirror (of a discriminatory social order). It is dangerous to assume that these eyes necessarily conceal a peaceful interlocutor.

Metaphysics does for Levinas's face what ontology does for anxiety, boredom, and wonder in Heidegger: it transforms a mundane event into a powerful philosophical concept. But it does so at the price of entering it into a conceptual system which abstracts from the everyday functioning of discriminatory practices. Levinas, no less than Plato, Heidegger, or Hegel is a systematic thinker. The nodes of his conceptual web can be enumerated by anyone who reads him critically. This means that

Levinas is guilty of the same charge he levels at Heidegger: ontology-building. But Levinas supplements his ontology with a theological ground, so as not to diminish its ethical import. This means, in my view, that we must be wary of what the eyes of the Other command. The face is not necessarily an unequivocal phenomenon, but it can be constituted as such, and arguably always is—our faces often give us away, operating as they do as the differential that faithfully interpellates us ("ambushes" us, as George Yancy would say)[22] in the racial order. This is the danger of Levinas's ontology.

The face betrays its real significance, both its equivocal and unequivocal contours, if and only if we notice the "color" (race, gender, class, etc.) of its eyes, its skin, and its command. Ethics is always bound on one side by an imperative to do justice to the particularity of the Other and on the other side by the motivation to see in him or her the common goodness in everyone. This is the double-bind imposed on us by the *actuality* of real ethical problems, which are always refracted through a complex socio-historical lens and which resist reduction to any ahistorical formula. Specifically, as Patricia Williams has put it, "This tension between material conditions and what one is cultured to see or not see...is a tension faced by any society driven by bitter histories of imposed hierarchy."[23] Forsaking either of these elements, the particular/historical or the universal, releases us from the basic tension and inevitable complexity that makes ethical matters so difficult to resolve.

Bernasconi contends that Levinas's remark about the color of the Other's eyes is not meant as a practical injunction and should not be taken as a dismissal of the ethical valence of the phenomenal characteristics that identify someone as a member of a particular (racial, ethnic, religious, etc.) group. Rather, it is meant to suggest that it is incumbent upon *us* not to allow the generalized social markings of the Other to efface the singular interruption that every Other introduces into the social order. As

Bernasconi says, singularity should be understood "not as a phenomenon that can be unveiled, but as an enigma."[24] But it could be argued that enigmas are practically unsatisfactory and leave too much to presumption, a loyal ally of discrimination. To allow the Other to remain enigmatic and absolutely beyond recognition—as Levinas must, since this is what makes his philosophy innovative—is to claim that the imperative the Other commands issues from elsewhere, from some unmarked locale. That is, some place where my body cannot be and therefore cannot hear.[25] How do I even begin to respond appropriately to such a call? When the alterity of the Other is deemed absolute, we overlook the fact that racism often thrives on such a disregard for the phenomenality of the face; it "bypasses the attachment to social identity that is often found on the part of the oppressed"[26] and leaves us paralyzed, awaiting the revelation that will enable us to respond. It seems to me that Levinas ought to have made the color of the Other's eyes—along with the rest of his/her phenomenal features—an essential feature of the Other's singularity. Even if he does not completely dismiss such features, Levinas does not attribute enough significance to the phenomenal in his account of faciality. I will now try to make good on this criticism.

Hyperbole of the Face

The face breaks up the totality of being, bursts apart the order of appearance and phenomenality. This breakup is the institution of divine law, the ethical command. Levinas's face has no gender or race; it is beyond human aspects; it does not contort with exasperation or fear, its speech is rendered voiceless—the Other disappears into a world without qualities or coordinates, beyond recognition and beyond immediate contact. With one exception: Levinas says that it is at the level of discourse or speech that we remain bound to the Other. Discourse—i.e., a "discourse before discourse"—is presupposed as the *sine qua non* of human relation. "Better than comprehension," Levinas says, "*discourse* relates with what remains essentially transcendent."[27] Speech reaches through the phenomenality of the face and introduces the Other.[28] Or, more precisely, the condition of speech accomplishes this. As Peperzak puts it, in speech "I address myself to another person who reveals that my monopoly has come to an end. [The Other] robs me of my sovereignty, but thereby frees me from solitude."[29] Speech presupposes my debt of freedom to the Other, which I am made to answer for when the Other approaches. This is the performative value proper to the face, and what makes its speech an inescapable—because transcendental—imperative.

Speech, the primordial ethical bond which comes before any ontology of intersubjectivity or *Mitsein*, is a language that no one can hear or listen to. Speech has no distinct graphical or phonetic marks; it lacks a certain timbre or pitch, a discrete dialect, diction, or slang. Reading Levinas, discourse and speech come off as either pure formalities or the mute pronouncements of a God who may or may not speak to us any longer. Moreover, "discourse" seems to contain a troubling paradox. If Levinas's discourse (in text and concept) is of a monotheistic propriety (Judeo-Christianity), does it not belong to a discursive regime that remains deaf to pagan, polytheistic, and atheistic interventions, which is to say, *to the other discourses which both enable and contest it as its other*? If so, three questions arise: first, given this paradox, what might be the legitimating authority which nevertheless underwrites the performativity of the face? Might not the imperative power of speech be located elsewhere? Second, are we ready to concede that a transcendental speech, a language prior to the inarticulate stammering of a voice in distress, is what charges the face with its moral significance? Third, is the transcendental value of Levinas's conception of discourse not undone by the religious discourse from which it issues?

What Levinas identifies as Saying, which opposes itself to the dead letter of the Said, is meant to breathe life into the formal structure[30] of discourse and rational dialogue.[31] This is why in *Otherwise than Being*, he writes that: "Signification, the one-for-the-other, has meaning only among beings of flesh and blood."[32] Saying, in its materiality, indicates the corporeal form of communication, the first-personal appeal that the Other makes upon us—I hasten to add, through the corporeal phenomenon of the voice[33]—when it addresses us face-to-face. It must be suggested, however, that the privilege granted to Saying in *Otherwise than Being* is compromised by the superhuman status afforded the face in *Totality and Infinity*. This draws our attention back to the problematic elevation of the concept of the face, which Deleuze and Guattari can help us understand in their critique of faciality in *A Thousand Plateaus*. We will return to this in a moment.

Levinas needs to hyperbolize the face in order to buttress his thinking of the Other. Why is this? Because the face must express, above all else, the command not to kill. And this command, this moral law, as we know, does not resonate with us as an absolute unless it issues from God. Failing that, the moral law must be given some other transcendental significance. *Otherwise than Being* displays Levinas's attempt to find this other ground. This is one of Levinas's most substantial innovations, one which seems to have become necessary for ethics to resume in the wake of Nietzsche. The divine command certainly does not come out of the ontological horizon of Heidegger, which only admits what can be brought into the light and comprehended. God and His Word are exempt from this display, so ethical truth must be revealed otherwise. Levinas entrusts the face to present us with the ethical command that always already sustains us. Discourse carries the divine Word which gives the face its immediate ethical meaning and is presupposed by any horizon of understanding. It is what allows us to apprehend the truest meaning of the Other and to know the "temptation and impossibility" of killing the Other. All of this transpires precisely because my freedom and power to kill is made possible by the nourishment the Other has always already provided for me. The transcendental character of the Other, then, places it beyond any historicized act of violence which I might commit.[34]

Impotent Violence

We catch a glimpse of the sensuous form of the Other's imperative, and Levinas's supersession of its features, when he problematizes the murderous act. He needs the face of the Other to be the revelation of an exteriority beyond comprehension, beyond freedom, and beyond dialogue. The Other becomes the condition of possibility for knowledge, action, and communication. The face must become the expression of transcendence if it is going to systematically dismantle the power of a violence that would harm, or worse, destroy the Other. He thus makes the ontology of freedom dependent upon the ethics of alterity.

Levinas's ethics dissolves the power of the murderer by making the act of murder illogical, literally without sense, and therefore powerless.[35] The murderer does not realize that he has been rendered passive before the Other. Every attempt to murder becomes, in Levinas's eyes, a senseless and impotent act, one that completely misunderstands the metaphysics of intersubjectivity.[36] This is because what the murderer intends to destroy is beyond the scope of intentionality and cannot be represented, much less seized; the hatred or contempt which is felt by the murderer is always mistaken, directed at an Other whose reality resides beyond the reach of violence. The command not to kill comes from beyond the totality of intentional acts and references.[37] This account of the Other should give us pause. It requires us to admit that the one we love or despise is not the one we see, embrace, or curse. *That* person is just a façade, our contact with them a dissimulation. Can we trust this person? It seems that for Levinas we *must*. But does this mean that the killing of another person is an illusion? If so, what is the meaning of murder, beyond a failure to accomplish a violent contact? The metaphysics of murder evinces the importance of hospitality. The exigency of the unconditional hospitality advocated by Levinas cannot be dismissed, but it also cannot be uncritically accepted or delved into here. It must suffice for us to consider a conditional form of hospitality toward the phenomenon of the face.[38]

The problem of the authenticity and authority of the command, as well as the ontotheological account of the Other, can be circumvented if we prioritize the face in its material expression. Would not the difficulty of killing another who looks straight into your eyes be enough to call you, the would-be murderer, into question? Levinas says as much in "Philosophy and the Idea of Infinity": the Other "can also...oppose himself to me beyond all measure, with the total uncoveredness and nakedness of his defenseless eyes, the straightforwardness, the absolute frankness of his gaze."[39] At this moment Levinas finds the Other not in the face, but in the vulnerable mortality of the eyes. But despite his acknowledgement of the affective recoil induced in an executioner when he or she witnesses the facial expressions of the condemned, Levinas finds it necessary to once again go beyond the expressive surface of the eyes. He dislocates expressivity from its immanence and, in the case of murder, dissociates it from the imminence of bodily death. This gesture of transcendence is unnecessary: Levinas acknowledges that the employment of execution-style killing testifies to the adequacy of the face in its singularity and specificity. In the execution, the executioner is hooded or the condemned is turned away—in both scenarios, no facial expressions are exchanged between murderer and murdered. The contours of the face speak a language all their own, a language more textured than the "epiphany" of discourse. This language is not lacking in practical effects.

Facial Deviance and Racial Deviants

The divine command of the face provokes a host of questions regarding the authenticity of the divine voice, and the authority of the one summoned, that Kierkegaard famously depicts (and Derrida scrutinizes in *The Gift of Death*) in his portrayal of Abraham's dilemma in *Fear and Trembling*. Augustine already captures the problematic in his *Soliloquies*, when he writes: "Of a sudden, someone spoke to me—perhaps it was myself, perhaps some other, outside me or within, I do not know."[40] The problem of authenticity notwithstanding, when raised to the level of the Absolute, which inevitably means absolute standard, the face presents us with a whole series of problems which we will call problems of *facial deviance*. Levinas's contention that the face is a revelation shows its weakness when confronted by race and feminist philosophies. This is where we see his ethical metaphysics contested by an infinity of complexions which Levinas has to subsume, for "economic" reasons, under a single ethical principle: *the* face. Deleuze and Guattari begin to unpack facial deviance in a chapter from *A Thousand Plateaus* entitled "Year Zero: Faciality." We should digest their criticism before reappraising faciality.

The face, for Deleuze and Guattari, operates as a transcendental signifier that opens a semiotic system tyrannized by the face of Christ. The face of Christ acts as a normative horizon in the racial and moral registers. "The face is not a universal," they say. "It is not even that of the white man; it is White Man himself, with his broad cheeks and the black holes of his eyes. The face is Christ."[41] The face, for Deleuze and Guattari, acts as a violent and oppressive sign that calls to order, with a univocal pronouncement, the command of the white man, authorized as he is by his resemblance to the Christian Savior. What they intend to adduce through this metonymy is the historical presence of a racial order supported by sociopolitical, religious, economic, and metaphysical components which always lead us back into the colonialism of the West and its normative horizon.[42]

In one capacity, the face institutes a hegemonic order that measures otherness according to a centralized standard: the white, male, European face. The "light" and the "dark" are indexed to this norm. "If the face is in fact Christ, in other words, your average ordinary White Man, then the first deviances...are racial: yellow man, black man, men in the second or third category."[43] Critical race theorist George Yancy amplifies this point in his reading of Toni Morrison's *The Bluest Eye*. Under Yancy's reading, the "blue eyes" of the white man—a signifier which functions as metonymically in the racial register as "Christ" does for Deleuze and Guattari—enact on the black body "the normalizing disciplinary techniques of whiteness," rendering it "ugly" in its very blackness when measured against the universal beauty of whiteness.[44] As Yancy might put it, the body of the black man is reflected back upon him by the blue-eyed gaze of the white man or woman, thus returning his black body to him with a "deviant" valuation. The references to Foucault are explicit here,[45] and they alert us to the danger which lurks in the eyes of the Other, especially when the complexion of those eyes reflect an oppressive or violent power/knowledge regime. This is why in order to combat racism *it is necessary to notice the color of the Other's eyes*, and above all not to pretend as though there is no color to be seen! There is a whole ethics of facial recognition/profiling here. Moreover, as Yancy shows, it is necessary to uncover (genealogically, he would say) the field of possibilities that lay beneath the "façade of whiteness" and the subtle ways it influences the construction of non-white, non-male, and non-Western identities, and reinforces whiteness as a value code.[46]

The face *cannot* appear differently in a globalized community animated by the sociopolitical and racial vicissitudes of the West. It is made to function as a reinforcement of the dominant order, not as a sign of this order's instability or equivocity. For Deleuze and Guattari, the face, in as much as it is complicit in the racial privilege of white men, "operates by the determination of degrees of deviance in relation to the White-Man face...which never abides alterity."[47] This is the "inhumanity" and the "horror" of the face—its tendency to signify, without equivocation, the infinity that is the God of Western white man and *His* commandments. The point is to escape the univocity of the face, to dismantle or resignify the system of facial deviance, and to "detect the particles of the other"[48] without entering them into the racist's order of expression. In short, when we fail to see the "color" which is written[49] all over the face, we blind ourselves to the racially charged matrices of power/knowledge that are reinforced, but also potentially undone, in our face-to-face interactions. Color-blindness of this type renders us unequipped to read and resist those powers.

Sensitivity of/to the Face

A different face is needed. If we allow Levinas's face to interrupt the phenomenal order,[50] to install an ethical order which derives its authority from the "noumenal glory"[51] of the Other, then we sacrifice the phenomenality of the ethical imperative and reduce its possible manifestations to one—the revelation of God—when in reality the number of possible imperatives is effectively infinite. This reduction is, at the phenomenal level, impossible and should be rejected as irrational and unnecessary, despite its resemblance to Kantianism. The fact that there are an indefinite number of actual faces that make a claim on my ethical sensibility is enough to render the infinity of God redundant, redundancy being one of the primary tactics of domination.[52] When the face of God supervenes on the visage of the other (now decapitalized), it neglects the indelible force exerted by other bodies on our own. We forget that it is not just reason and revelation that disrupts our totality, but sensation and the sensuousness/sensuality of the face.

"Sensation is the break-up of every system," says Levinas.[53] Sensation, like speech, he gives a transcendental function, which seems to me a more compelling basis for his ethics.[54] This means that ethics is, and must be, a corporeal matter; the imperative is received not only by our rational faculties, but by our carnal sensibility, which is fundamentally an affective capacity and an irreducible component of intercorporeal survival. Our responsiveness to other bodies, which at once conditions our sensitive responsibility to them, is anterior to our competent manipulation of tools within a system of equipment, instruments, and projects. [55] To sense the other and be sensitive to them is a condition for stabilizing our own bodies within the world and figuring out how to work with others toward a pluralistic future.

Our carnal sensibility, which meets with the face of the other in all its unfathomable complexity and its sensuous complexion, does not require the formalism of Kantian morality to find itself summoned to responsibility. This summons issues from the naked materiality that the other presents to us, a materiality that is elemental and, as such, ungraspable. This materiality is "what has consistency, weight, is absurd, is a brute but impassive presence; it is also what is humble, bare and ugly." The face of the other signifies the sheer fact of existence which burdens each one of us; "matter is the very fact of the *there is...*," Levinas says in *Existence and Existents*.[56] This fact is written on the body of the other, is discernible in the scars and laugh lines, crow's feet and fatigued countenance of the other. This is a metaphysical point, not an empirical one. Whether we respond to these features or to the faceless ego behind the eyes determines how we apprehend the humanity of the other. And why not locate the singularity of the other in his or her material complexity, as Foucault suggests? The face of the other would then be apprehended as the site of an event, a "play of dominations" where power, memories, and rituals are engraved.[57] In Michel Tournier's words, the face is the part of our flesh which is endlessly molded and remolded, warmed, animated by the presence of our fellows. After parting from someone with whom he has had an animated conversation, a man's face retains a glow which only gradually fades and may be rekindled if he meets someone else.[58]

The contorted or radiant animation of the face eludes precise calculation. It is invested by a certain encounter, or confluence of encounters, that could never be untangled. Do not the histories of our bodies differentiate us to a sufficient degree, to the point of individuating us within the formless matter of the *il y a* and placing our "subjectivity" beyond the understanding of any possible interlocutor? Ethics would then entail a passive respect for this complex history, an unwillingness to impose a familiar form on the "humble, bare and ugly" materiality of the face or to compromise its integrity. An ethics of this sort would not require us to recognize the divine beauty which radiates from beyond the fleshy gaze of a stranger, but would proscribe violence toward the "absurd ugliness" of that stranger. Aesthetics would come to displace the priority of ethics. Levinas himself is not unaccustomed to conceiving ethics as reverential aesthetics.

Deviations of Faciality

Few have done more to draw out the importance of sensation and sensibility for Levinas's ethics than Alphonso Lingis. As a reader of Levinas, Lingis has both adopted Levinas's ethical injunction and modified it to lend due consideration to the aesthetic singularity of the face. On this score, Lingis's texts bring to light the injustice involved in the effacement of another's guise. The ethical imperative, for Lingis, is embedded in the phenomenality of beings, not in the noumenal or divine sphere. Turn to the opening page of any chapter in Lingis's texts: there you will find a smiling, stoic, or, above all, *sincere* face looking back at you—an imperative staring you down in the dignified form of a Brazilian street kid or a Guatemalan mother with her child slung over her back. Lingis tries to convey the unique experiences undergone by some encounter with a foreigner in a strange land or unfamiliar locale. He has developed a knack for conveying the inexpressible character of these encounters, for giving voice to the faces that defy representation. This is not because these faces lack their own expressivity or are somehow beyond recognition. They do not present his camera with exotic and alien visages whose humanity is unidentifiable and must be explained. It is simply that Lingis's camera will always fail to capture the complex of memories, fantasies, codes, incapacities, abilities, and obligations that that coalesce in the face of his subjects. Of necessity he must annotate his photographs.

Each of these complexes are gathered in the body of the other, the concrete site of the other's humanity: it is what constitutes the tangible "you" with whom we make contact.[59] The phenomenon of trust testifies to this contact, for when we trust we "attach to someone whose words or whose movements we do not understand, whose reasons or motives we do not see."[60] Despite our failures, we do not turn away or abandon our desire to engage the other. Our trust answers to a dare, not an obligation. It rides on the contingency of responsibility. We catch on to the other's voice and allow its unmistakable appeal to solicit our effortless interlocution. Because the laughter or tears of another are *contagious*, the other becomes a magnet for us or reflects in their eyes our own mortality.[61] This is the kind of non-allergic contact which Levinas desires, but it is not a contact which can be prescribed. We can always flee the scene and head home. Our sensibility is attracted to or is repulsed by the visage of the other; our trust or distrust follows on the heels of this corporeal proximity. "Our trust," Lingis writes, "short-circuits across the space where we represent socially defined behaviors and makes contact with the real individual agent there—with *you*."[62] If such contact were impossible, would it not also be impossible to recognize others' gestures and respond to their solicitations as directed to us? Would it not be impossible even to consider placing our faith in this other individual? It is the experience of real, immanent contact with the other that, despite Levinas's contestations, must be rehabilitated in our consideration of ethics in general and of the face-to-face relation particularly. The point is to conceive this contact not at the level of cognitive recognition or identification, but at the level of a precarious affectivity or carnal sensibility.[63] Responsibility is much less a somber obligation than it is an exhilarating risk.

Lingis's phenomenological travel writing exemplifies the type of non-cognitive ethical sensibility I am advocating.[64] His ethical sensibility is nourished by and grounded in the face-to-face contact which constitutes the foundation of his travels. Travels which, incidentally, perform a kind of "autobiographical refutation" of Kantian morality: Lingis's ethics is borne of his countless excursions across the globe, whereas the categorical imperative is the invention of a man who never left his hometown.[65] An imperative turns up in Lingis's writings which is prior to language, but not prior to the senses of travel. It occurs between beings who do not share the same language, but who somehow make sense of each other. To make sense of that other becomes our responsibility. A voice, not just a sound, enters my ear. "The words have penetrated right through the role, the social identity, the visible and interpretable form, to the very core that is me."[66] *Someone has spoken to me; they have contacted me. I will attempt to respond:* "A slum dweller in Brazil, after a mudslide or the polluting of his water supply, who reaches out to me reaches out for the skills and resources of my hands. [...] The fatigue, the vertigo, the homelessness in his body appeal first for terrestrial support from my body which stands steady on the earth."[67] The voice makes sense to us, indicates to us a unique face who appeals to our material well-being. "Beneath the face as a surface for signs," Lingis writes,

> we see the skin in its carnality and vulnerability. We see in the spasms, the wrinkles, the wounds on her skin, the urgency of her hunger, her thirst, her cold, her fever, her fear, or her despair. We are immediately afflicted with these wounds, these wants, this suffering. In our hands extended to clasp her hands, touch turns to tact and tenderness.[68]

Our response to the other does not first pass through the existential structures of being, but neither does it pass through the authority of God. As Lingis insists, our responsibility is triggered immediately by the corporeality of the other: "We cannot view the sufferer's contorted hands, his grimaces, hear his sighs and moans, without these inducing contortions, grimaces, sighs, and moans in us, and with them, inducing a sense of the pain."[69] Our response to the other is first and foremost the incontestable response of our bodies to the imperative that only our bodies can detect. The face of the other is the face of every other, an infinity of others whose sensuousness claims us. Lingis's travel writing performs an ethics of the body by responding impossibly to the complexity and excess of faces, without effacing the determinate location in which those faces appear.[70] In this way he enacts the Levinasian ethic and its impossible demand—an impossibility which is indigenous to the exigency of ethics.

The danger, of course, is that the sense made of the foreigner's face will reflect the white, male, Western, hegemonic complex of values that Lingis carries with him in his physiognomy and comportment. He has confessed a personal apprehensiveness about photographing others and the potential for deformation in such images.[71] There is certainly an irresponsible form of travel, one that does violence to the other by scrutinizing their world in the light of our own and pretending that our perceptual competence is adequate to theirs. This is why it is necessary—and I do not believe that Lingis would see things otherwise—to actively practice what María Lugones calls "world-traveling," in which, as Shannon Sullivan puts it, "one allows for a pluralistic world and a complex picture of how common meaning is forged out of, but does not necessarily eliminate, different perspectives and interests."[72] World-traveling denotes a form of identification that substitutes playful, loving perception for the "arrogant perception" that judges the other according to the categories of the same.

World-traveling can act as a short-circuit to what Sullivan calls "ontological expansiveness," a concept that shares Levinas's anxiety over the totalizing tendencies of formal thought, but which also goes beyond Levinas in significant ways. Ontological expansiveness, for Sullivan, refers to the way in which privileged races and cultures are capable of extending their territory by assimilating the territory of the other. It is the expansion of a world and a place where one will, in Lugones's terms, "feel at ease," thus bringing *dis*-ease to the territory one colonizes. In Sullivan's words, "As ontologically expansive, white people consider all spaces as rightfully available for their inhabitation of them. A white person's choice to change her environment in order to challenge her unconscious habits of white privilege can be just another instance of ontological expansiveness."[73]

Ontological expansiveness obviously leads white folks into a catch-22: as racially privileged, they take for granted their comfort within and mobility through space. To undo this privilege it is necessary to move between worlds and travel into other territories with the hope of undoing their unconscious habits. Violence against the other appears inevitable. It seems to me that the notions of white privilege and habit which Sullivan describes could exemplify the kind of violence that Levinas believes to be inherent in sociality. Whether his generalization of violence eliminates its cultural and racial specificity is an open question. Sullivan suggests that there might be ways to consciously escape the (often unconscious) violence of white privilege. Basically, this means changing one's environment, world-traveling, and hoping "that the changed environment will help produce an improved habit in its place."[74] Another paradox arises: in order to conduct world-traveling, it is necessary to have already overcome ontologically expansive behavior, thus preserving the plurality of worlds that could be traveled to. It appears that a certain degree of passivity or spontaneity is key to combating ontological expansiveness, its operation being so elusive, so microscopic.

The dangers involved in ontological expansiveness, arrogant perception, and irresponsible travel summon Levinas's injunction to hospitality. But they also alert us to the virtues of *chance*. When we find ourselves in a world that is not our own, and our desire is not to commit violence, but to understand that world, then it is necessary to respond to that world passively, to minimize our determinations on the scene. The passivity of responsibility describes a welcoming of exposure (to the other), come what may. It is neither agonistic nor dialectical. Instead, it is playful: "Given the agonistic attitude," Lugones says, "one *cannot* travel across 'worlds', though can kill other 'worlds' with it. So for people who are interested in crossing racial and ethnic boundaries, an arrogant western man's construction of playfulness [as agonistic] is deadly."[75] Playfulness describes the renunciation of praktognosis, the practical and perceptual mastery that sometimes gets the best of Merleau-Ponty's thinking of alterity.[76] The language of play connotes a floating signification, which contrasts the transcendental, religious "discourse" of Levinas. In play identities are free to try each other out or borrow from one another. Playfulness is a more mundane attitude toward the other than the "religion" prescribed by Levinas, but nevertheless it is consonant with his aversion to agonism. It offers a transactional encounter which is responsible but not completely passive, which improvises engagement with the other without sacrificing the worlds brought into the fold.

Alterity without Revelation

In sum, I think Levinas misreads the face-to-face encounter to the extent that he understands the façade of the face as superfluous to ethical relations. It is not for him the face "in the flesh" that presents the ethical relation, but something behind and above the face. Of course, it is much more efficient for him to defend this claim, instead of confronting the infinity of singular faces that constitute the plurality of the population. Levinas has to settle for efficiency (by which I mean a certain level of generality) if his ethics is going to get off the ground. And, indeed, even though the autobiographical style taken up by Lingis and many philosophers of race seems more suitable to the "thickness" of the face-to-face encounter, Levinas's metaphysical mode does lend a certain "depth" to the hyper-historical testimonial. Even social constructionist or narrative theories of the self require an ontological depth, the kind of depth which ontological analyses of "facticity" or "worldhood" lend to notions like "location," "situatedness," and "embodiment." Levinas provides some of this depth.

Levinas's ontology commits him to a humanism which sees in social relations the meeting of souls, or self-identical persons. This is what divine otherness comes to. When I love another person or despise them, it is something inalienable and essential that I intend—this is the "glory of the noumenal." But we need not spiritualize the other or presume some transcendent existent beyond the face to uphold a certain humanism of the other; indeed, as we have seen, it is dangerous to do so and such presumption forecloses certain possibilities for world-traveling. I have tried to suggest that another Levinas is legible in his texts, one that Lingis consistently reads. There is enough in the contours of the face, the hue of the skin, and the sparkle of the eyes to interrupt violence without having to appeal to divine command. The mundane is excessive enough to dislocate totality. Levinas knows as much; the defense of materiality that makes up his critique of transcendental egoism betrays this knowledge. His entire description of the ontogenesis of the self in *Totality and Infinity*, not to mention his description of the subject's enigmatic harassment by the *il y a* in *Existence and Existents*, is grounded in a materialist ontology of the mundane. It is here that we would locate the element of chance latent in Levinas's ethics.[77]

Under this reading the absence of sensation in Heidegger and Hegel would be what is truly objectionable about their ontologies. Sensation is an epistemological excess. It opens onto an infinity that relentlessly impresses upon us, calibrating our motility while at the same time threatening to transgress our cognitive and practical thresholds with sublimity and fatigue. Is it not the relegation of sensation to the status of an epistemological unknown in Kantian idealism, for instance, that Levinas ultimately sees as presumptuous? Heidegger ignores sensation; Hegel sublates it. In both cases the sensuous is tamed. This is what Lugones means to criticize with the notion of "arrogant perception." But Heidegger at least recognizes the ontological significance of the affective dimension of being-in-the-world, which Levinas acknowledges as an essential component of ethical sensibility. The return of sensation and its affective dimension in Levinas's ontology, it seems to me, is what allows his thinking of the other to escape closure, precisely because sensation is what allows us to make contact with exteriority without subjecting that exteriority to our representational devices. Sensation is unforeseeable and commands a response; it enables and disables, and thus has an unruliness built into it that the body must negotiate with.

Levinas transgresses the sensuousness of the face by making

it speak the divine Word. In this way he forces a meaning on the other and reinforces a semiotics that might otherwise be contested by the singular voices of the face. This semiotics, as we have seen, is preprogrammed, and the face is readily enlisted in its circulation. This is why I want to end by suggesting that Levinas's description of the *nape* offers a less violent object than the face in our exploration of the vulnerability of the other—for the nape presents us with an immanent and non-signifying sensuality that, paradoxically, signifies non-violence. The passivity of the nape requires no transcendental obligation to transform it into an imperative. In the nape, Levinas says, "all the weakness, all the mortality, all the naked and disarmed mortality of the other can be read from it."[78] In this way, the nape "functions" as the face, Levinas says. But by insisting that the nape functions as a face, Levinas forces the nape back into a system of reference that overrides the nape's immanent prohibitions, when it should in fact be seen as contesting the semiotics of the face and its standards of beauty. This is the prime violence of Levinas's metaphysical system. Against this, we might insist that the bare, defenseless texture of the back of another's neck works autonomously to dismantle the hegemony of the face, and paralyzes violence in the web of passions triggered by the fragility reflected in that disarming surface.

Notes

1. In his paper "Rereading *Totality and Infinity*," in *The Question of the Other: Essays in Contemporary Continental Philosophy*, eds. Arleen B. Dallery and Charles E. Scott (Albany: SUNY Press, 1989), Bernasconi contrasts the empiricist and transcendental readings of Levinas. The former emphasizes the concreteness of the face-to-face relation while the latter highlights the role of the transcendent Other (human) in the constitution of the Same, or ego-centered subjectivity. Here I am defending the empiricist reading, but I do not oppose the

transcendental reading. In fact, I am interested in working out a position that combines these two readings, what would amount to a "transcendental empiricist" reading of Levinas that privileges what he calls the "transcendental function" of sensation. On my reading sensation becomes the term which links Same and Other, acting as both an enabling and disabling condition of possibility.

2. Emmanuel Levinas, *Totality and Infinity*, trans. Alphonso Lingis (Pittsburgh: Duquesne University Press, 1969), 66.

3. The link between totality and politics can be easily gleaned from chapter 6 of Emmanuel Levinas, *Ethics and Infinity*, trans. Richard A. Cohen (Pittsburgh: Duquesne University Press, 1985).

4. Emmanuel Levinas, "Philosophy and the Idea of Infinity," in *Collected Philosophical Papers*, trans. Alphonso Lingis (Pittsburgh: Duquesne University Press, 1987), 52.

5. This is what is implied in the analyses of the overtly Heideggerian themes of habitation, home, work, and dwelling in Section II of *Totality and Infinity*. Each of these themes can be shown to refer back to the immanence of the *Da* of Dasein, which for Levinas signifies the insulated world of the Same. The interruption of the world which the transcendence of the other enacts is absent from the Heideggerian system because the other is not a transcendence, but a participant in the immanent structures of Dasein's existence.

6. Levinas, *Totality and Infinity*, 67.

7. Jean-Luc Marion, "The Intentionality of Love," in *Prolegomena to Charity*, trans. Stephen Lewis (New York: Fordham University Press, 2002), 82. The essay from which this citation comes is an "homage" to Levinas.

8. Adriaan Peperzak, *To the Other: An Introduction to the Philosophy of Emmanuel Levinas* (West Lafayette, IN: Purdue University Press, 1993), 164

9. Note the emphasis placed on "receiving" the infinite in Levinas, *Totality and Infinity*, 204.

10. Anticipating a bit, it should be said that, although Levinas recognizes an asymmetry in the I-Thou relation, this asymmetry explicitly refers us to the divinity, or "Height," of the face, but fails to attend to the asymmetry that derives from socioeconomic inequalities. Qualifying Buber, George Yancy reminds us: "This I-Thou interpersonal relationship... is always already structured by other social positions and locations such as class, race, and gender. The 'I' is always already located in its encounter with the 'thou', which is also always already located and shaped within a larger social matrix of other dynamic transversal locations." See "Introduction: Philosophy and the Situated Narrative Self," in *The Philosophical I: Personal Reflections on Life in Philosophy*, ed. George Yancy (Lanham, MD: Rowman and Littlefield, 2002), xx.

11. Others are encountered for Heidegger within a context of equipment. "They are encountered from out of the *world*, in which concernfully circumspective Dasein essentially dwells." This means that others are encountered not as wholly other beings, but as beings who are pre-understood insofar as they participate in and share a world with me. This world is structured for the other and myself by our common *concern* for being-in-the-world. For Levinas all of this boils down to the fact that Dasein's contact with others is always mediated by its ontological structure, the structure of care. Cf. Martin Heidegger, *Being and Time*, trans. John Macquarrie and Edward Robinson (San Francisco: HarperCollins, 1962), §26.

12. Hannah Arendt, "Labor, Work, Action," in *The Portable Hannah Arendt*, ed. Eric Baehr (New York: Viking, 2000), 179-180.

13. Levinas, *Totality and Infinity*, 46.

14. For Levinas's theses against Heidegger, see *Totality and Infinity*, 45. "Justice" in this context is concerned with making us responsible for the unforeseeable effects of our actions, those which extend beyond our intimate relations and into the world of "the third." It signifies the anteriority of heteronomy to autonomy, and is the first principle of ethics as first philosophy. As Edith Wyschogrod has put it in *Emmanuel Levinas: The Problem of Ethical Metaphysics* (The Hague: Martinus Nijhoff, 1974), 99: "Our transgression against another is thrown out of kilter, falsified, as it were, by the other's relation with a third, a relation which may well be unknown to us. Since we cannot calculate the other's relation to the third, that third may be injured by our receiving pardon [from more intimate others]." Heidegger's conceptions of freedom and being-with are incapable of comprehending this triadic relation and the form of responsibility which arises within it. This is because, for Levinas, he never stops to consider the conditions under which freedom is enabled by the alterity of the other.

15. Cf. Emmanuel Levinas, "Is Ontology Fundamental?", in *Entre Nous: Thinking-of-the-Other*, trans. Michael B. Smith and Barbara Harshav (New York: Columbia University Press, 1998), 10.

16. Wyschogrod, *Emmanuel Levinas*, 85.

17. Levinas, *Totality and Infinity*, 199.

18. Levinas, *Ethics and Infinity*, 85.

19. Levinas, *Totality and Infinity*, 66.

20. Marion, "The Intentionality of Love," 81.

21. This is basically a Foucauldian point, taken from the Introduction to Volume I of the *History of Sexuality*, trans. Robert Hurley (New York: Vintage, 1978), which demonstrates that what we call "freedom," no less than what we call "subjection," is necessarily produced by the coercive powers and social forces which shape us. These forces, for

Foucault, are material in their physiological and psychological functions, but they are not distinct from abstract or immaterial conceptual matrices. Subjectivity would be unthinkable were it not for this tandem of forces. The process of subjectification can spin out of control, however, and the "black holes" of the Other's eyes can become the very maelström in which one's subjectivity is obliterated. This notion, which cuts against the grain of Marion and Levinas, is drawn out nearly term for term by Deleuze and Guattari in their analysis of faciality, which is taken up summarily below.

22. See George Yancy, *Black Bodies, White Gazes* (Lanham, MD: Rowman and Littlefield, 2008), chapter 7. Incidentally, "ambush" is the term Levinas employs to characterize the nature of war. War is a contest in which one party seeks to overcome the strength of its adversary by exploiting the adversary's weakness. War is seeking out the Achilles' heel of the other. See Emmanueal Levinas, "Freedom and Command," in *Collected Philosophical Papers*, 19.

23. Patricia J. Williams, *Seeing a Color-Blind Future: The Paradox of Race* (New York: Noonday Press, 1998), 5.

24. Robert Bernasconi, "The Invisibility of Racial Minorities in the Public Realm of Appearances," in *Race*, ed. Robert Bernasconi (Malden, MA: Blackwell, 2001), 289.

25. The point here is Jean-Luc Nancy's, when he writes: "The idea of the ineffable always serves the cause of a higher, more secret, more silent, and more sublime word: a treasury of sense to which only those united with God have access. But 'God is dead' means: God no longer has a body." *The Birth to Presence*, trans. Brian Holmes et al. (Stanford: Stanford University Press, 1993), 190-191.

26. Bernasconi, "Invisibility," 290.

27. Levinas, *Totality and Infinity*, 195.

28. Levinas, *Totality and Infinity*, 193.

29. Adriaan Theodor Peperzak, *Beyond: The Philosophy of Emmanuel Levinas* (Evanston: Northwestern University Press, 1997), 12.

30. There are moments in *Totality and Infinity* (e.g., 195), as when Levinas says the following, where the very structure of language is sufficient for ethics: "The formal structure of language thereby announces the ethical inviolability of the Other and, without any odor of the 'numinous', his 'holiness'." This formalism seems to be precisely what is contested in the Saying/Said distinction drawn in *Otherwise than Being*. His penchant for the formal structures of inter-subjective relations, and his tendency to "ontologize" concrete categories—like fatigue, obsession, enjoyment, etc.—is evidence of Levinas's susceptibility to ontology, despite his protests against it. Levinas's susceptibility is, I take it, testimony to the inescapable primacy of ontology over ethics.

31. Simon Critchley gives a well-articulated exposition of the Saying/Said distinction, but he focuses more effort on adducing the ethical implications of the "performative" language of *Otherwise than Being*, and Levinas's increasingly deconstructive mode of operation, than he does on the material components of face-to-face expression and *their* ethical valence. I do not object to Critchley's reading of Levinasian ethics here; in fact, it is extremely compelling. But it underplays an entire dimension of Levinas's thinking in favor of now-familiar poststructuralist/deconstructive themes. Critchley's "Post-Deconstructive Subjectivity?", in *Ethics—Politics—Subjectivity* (London: Verso, 1999) does a much better job of illumining the materiality of sensibility. Now that the linguistic turn has subsided, we can begin to excavate the more tangible or "realist" components of Levinas's philosophy. See Simon Critchley, *The Ethics of Deconstruction: Derrida and Levinas*, second edition

(Edinburgh: Edinburgh University Press, 1999), 4-9.

32. Levinas, *Otherwise than Being*, 74.

33. I know of no more thoughtful treatment of the ethical and political significance of the voice than that carried out by Fred Evans, *The Multivoiced Body: Society and Communication in the Age of Diversity* (New York: Columbia University Press, 2009). Evans is vigilant in his critique of the "oracular" voices, such as that of the white supremacist, which persistently seek to silence the voices of otherness and assert their exclusionary truth. In my view Evans' attack on oracles is perfectly consonant with Deleuze and Guattari's criticism of the face and Lingis's treatment of the voice.

34. For this line of argument, see "Is Ontology Fundamental?", especially 9-11.

35. Levinas, "Philosophy and the Idea of Infinity," 55.

36. As Wyschogrod summarizes the metaphysics of murder: "The one who is killed is absolutely independent. [...] What we encounter is the infinity of his transcendence; his face is the expression of that infinity. The power of the infinite is stronger than the power of murder." *Emmanuel Levinas*, 86.

37. Levinas, "Philosophy and the Idea of Infinity," 55.

38. I am inclined to agree with Derrida and admit that the question of unconditional or absolute hospitality will always be an impure and undecidable, yet imperative, consideration. To dismiss the problem would lead to a deficient consideration of the other, but to adhere to its strictures could result in political negligence. As he writes in *Of Hospitality*, trans. Rachel Bowlby (Stanford: Stanford University Press, 2000), 135, "We will always be threatened by this dilemma between, on the one hand, unconditional hospitality that dispenses with law, duty, or even politics, and, on the other, hospitality circumscribed by law and duty. One of them can always corrupt the other, and this capacity for perversion remains irreducible. It *must* remain so."

39. Levinas, "Philosophy and the Idea of Infinity," 55.

40. Quoted in Peter Brown, *Augustine of Hippo: A Biography*, new edition (Berkeley: University of California Press, 2000), 111.

41. Gilles Deleuze and Félix Guattari, *A Thousand Plateaus*, trans. Brian Massumi (Minneapolis: University of Minnesota Press, 1987), 176.

42. For a balanced discussion of this point, see John Drabinski, *Levinas and the Postcolonial: Race, Nation, Other* (Edinburgh: Edinburgh University Press, 2011).

43. Deleuze and Guattari, *A Thousand Plateaus*, 178. Evidence of the historical presence of this scale of racial deviance, and its link to notions of universal beauty, is illustrated nicely in a remark by Goethe: "We venture, however,...to assert that the white man, that is, he whose surface varies from white to reddish, yellowish, brownish, in short, whose surface appears most neutral in hue and least inclines to any particular and positive colour, is the most beautiful." Quoted in George Yancy, "A Foucauldian (Genealogical) Reading of Whiteness: The Production of the Black Body/Self and the Racial Deformation of Pecola Breedlove in Toni Morrison's *The Bluest Eye*," in *What White Looks Like*, ed. George Yancy (London: Routledge, 2004), 119.

44. Yancy, "A Foucauldian (Genealogical) Reading of Whiteness," 109, 122.

45. In Foucault's terms: "The body is molded by a great many distinct regimes; it is broken down by the rhythms of work, rest and holidays; it is poisoned by food or values, through eating habits or moral laws; it constructs resistances." Michel Foucault, "Nietzsche, Genealogy, History," in *The Foucault Reader*, ed. Paul Rabinow (New York: Pantheon, 1984), 87.

46. Yancy, "A Foucauldian (Genealogical) Reading of Whiteness," 122, 137-138.

47. Deleuze and Guattari, *A Thousand Plateaus*, 178.

48. Deleuze and Guattari, *A Thousand Plateaus*, 178.

49. Foucault, "Nietzsche, Genealogy, History," 85.

50. Cf. Levinas, *Otherwise than Being*, 88.

51. Emmanuel Levinas, "The Ego and the Totality," in *Collected Philosophical Papers*, 43.

52. Deleuze and Guattari go so far as to say: "The face itself is redundancy." The face acts as a "loci of resonance," or a surface that reflects signifiers with a particular frequency and charge, thereby making language "conform in advance to a dominant reality." Faces are never wholly singular, but always define a particular degree of deviance from the dominant regime of signification, that is, the regime of the white man. Cf. *A Thousand Plateaus*, 168. Compare Yancy's position on the reflective power of the white gaze and its capacity to objectify or "return" the black body as "codified as *this* or *that* in terms of meanings that are sanctioned, scripted, and constituted through the processes of negotiation embedded within and serving various ideological interests, which are themselves grounded in deeper power-laden social processes. See "Whiteness and the Return of the Black Body," *Journal of Speculative Philosophy* 19, no. 4 (2005): 215-241.

53. Levinas, *Totality and Infinity*, 59.

54. Especially for the ethics of embodiment that we find in Levinas. On the transcendental role of sensation, see Levinas, *Totality and Infinity*, 188-189. See also Chapters 2 and 3 above.

55. This insight is gleaned from Lingis's marvelous text, *The Imperative* (Bloomington: Indiana University Press, 1998), which contributes significantly to our comprehension of the material basis of Levinas's ethics and offers a reformulated, corporeal version of the Kantian imperative.

56. Emmanuel Levinas, *Existence and Existents*, trans. Alphonso Lingis (The Hague: Martinus Nijhoff, 1978), 57.

57. See Foucault, "Nietzsche, Genealogy, History," 85.

58. Michel Tournier, *Friday*, trans. Norman Denny (New York: Pantheon, 1969), 86-87.

59. We cannot forget, to quote Foucault one last time, that this "humanity installs each of its violences in a system of rules and thus proceeds from domination to domination." "Nietzsche, Genealogy, History," 85.

60. Alphonso Lingis, *Trust* (Minneapolis: University of Minnesota Press, 2004), ix.

61. Alphonso Lingis, "Contact," *Janus Head* 8, no. 2 (2005): 439-454.

62. Lingis, *Trust*, ix.

63. The distinction between the cognitive/representational and the affective/non-intentional is elaborated in *Totality and Infinity*, particularly Section III, "Exteriority and the Face."

64. Levinas calls this "nonintentional consciousness," of which ethics is a privileged example. Nonintentional consciousness denotes the pre-thematic experiences of the lived body, the body whose contact with the concreteness of the lifeworld goes unnoticed and unreflected upon. Given his comments on sensation in *Totality and Infinity*, we could add sensing— specifically its affective or excessive dimension—to the forms of nonintentional consciousness. See his article, "Nonintentional Consciousness," in *Entre Nous*.

65. Perhaps the strangest thing in the anecdote about Kant having never left Königsberg is that Kant actually wrote one of the first texts of anthropology. As George Yancy has pointed out to me, in that text Kant gives an anthropological account of Africans, not one of whom Kant ever met. This leads me to speculate that Yancy's preference for the autobiographical mode of philosophical writing comes out of his antipathy toward Kant's anthropology and the way it reflects on his philosophical style. This is what brings Yancy close to Lingis and makes their philosophical *ethos* so different from traditional moral theory.

66. Lingis, "Contact," 441.
67. Lingis, *The Imperative*, 133.
68. Alphonso Lingis, *Dangerous Emotions* (Berkeley: University of California Press, 2000), 50.
69. Lingis, "Our Uncertain Compassion," *Janus Head* 9, no. 1 (2006): 25-32.
70. This reconciles Lingis's main criticism of Levinas's treatment of the face, which Lingis sees as ultimately sacrificing the singularity of the face to the monotheistic God who, for Levinas, is "constitutive of the otherness of the one who faces us...." For Lingis, this means that Levinas's face lacks determination, location, substance, and real difference. See Alphonso Lingis, "Objectivity and/of justice: A Critique of Emmanuel Levinas' Explanation," *Continental Philosophy Review* 32 (1999): 395-407.
71. See Mary Zourani, "Foreign Bodies: Interview with Alphonso Lingis," in *Encounters with Alphonso Lingis*, eds. Alexander E. Hooke and Wolfgang W. Fuchs (Lanham, MD: Lexington Books, 2003), 87-88.
72. Shannon Sullivan, *Living Across and Through Skins: Transactional Bodies, Pragmatism, and Feminism* (Bloomington: Indiana University Press, 2001), 79.
73. Shannon Sullivan, *Revealing Whiteness: The Unconscious Habits of White Privilege* (Bloomington: Indiana University Press, 2006), chapter 6.
74. Sullivan, *Revealing Whiteness*, Introduction.
75. María Lugones, "Playfulness, 'World'-Traveling, and Loving Perception," in *Making Face, Making Soul: Creative and Critical Perspectives by Feminists of Color*, ed. Gloria Anzaldua (San Francisco: Aunt Lute Books, 1990), 400.
76. Cf. Luce Irigaray's comments on the privileging of vision in Merleau-Ponty's later work, in *An Ethics of Sexual* Difference, trans. Carolyn Burke and Gillian C. Gill (Ithaca, NY: Cornell University Press, 193), 174. Sullivan echoes some of Irigaray's

concerns in *Living Across and Through Skins*, chapter 3. The attitude of playfulness lets go of the rules that typically guide interpersonal interactions and keep us in control of the situation. In play, "we are not worried about competence," says Lugones. This attitude is not incompatible with Levinas's; it is consonant with Levinas's metaphysics insofar as it is a metaphysics which expects the world to be "unruly" and beyond our finite capacity to gather the plurality of worlds into one "neat package" (Lugones, "Playfulness," 400).

77. Out of the ambivalent quality of sensation comes an ethics of the body that makes no appeal to the divine, but rather locates its imperative in the immanence of intercorporeal relations. Describing the play of chance in such an immanentist ontology would require some comparison of Levinasian metaphysics with what Louis Althusser has called "aleatory materialism." See Althusser's *Philosophy of the Encounter* (London: Verso, 2006).

78. Levinas, "The Other, Utopia, and Justice," in *Entre Nous*, 232.

6

Plastic Subjects[1]

A Synthetic Phenomenologist

Alphonso Lingis is well-known in the Anglophone world for his translations. Continental philosophers have all read his renderings of Levinas's *Totality and Infinity* and Merleau-Ponty's *The Visible and the Invisible*. He has also gained an admirable following with his philosophical travelogues, books like *Excesses*, *Abuses*, and *Trust*. In a way, even these texts offer us translations: of unfamiliar customs and peoples, of technical concepts and slippery philosophical jargon. In the travelogues readers witness phenomenological descriptions of individuals and cultures which are laced with the thinking of alterity familiar to Levinas's readers, and the phenomenology of the lived body that Merleau-Ponty has handed down to the continental tradition. Set either between or beyond these two notions—alterity and the lived body—is Lingis himself, a philosopher who not only builds a bridge between American and continental thought, but who is the literal embodiment of a synthetic brand of American continental philosophy. As if William James and Levinas were co-opted to author *all* of the guide books in the *Lonely Planet* series,[2] many of Lingis's hybrid books read like reports from the field. His missives from Latin and North America, Southeast Asia, Antarctica, Africa, and Europe set Lingis apart from the rest of the American philosophers working in Husserl's wake. His (inter)continental approach spans the globe and reaches beyond the technical skirmishes of academic philosophy. Diane Ackerman gives us a splendid caricature of Lingis's *modus operandi*:

Alphonso Lingis—whose unusual books, *Excesses* and *Libido*,

consider the realms of human sensuality and kinkiness—
travels the world sampling its exotic erotica. Often he primes
the pump by writing letters to friends. I possess some extra-
ordinary letters, half poetry, half anthropology, he sent me
from a Thai jail (where he took time out from picking vermin
to write), a convent in Ecuador, Africa (where he was scuba-
diving along the coast with filmmaker Leni Riefenstahl), and
Bali (where he was taking part in fertility rituals).[3]

The time is ripe for Lingis studies to be extended.[4]

By examining the subjectivity of Alphonso Lingis as
accounted for in his phenomenological writings, we can catch a
glimpse of his perspective on embodied subjectivity and its
relation to the sensible world. Following closely on the heels of
Levinas, Lingis sets philosophy in motion; his travel is phenomenology at work. This chapter articulates a few key dimensions
of Lingisian travel.

Lingis is a wanderer and a cosmopolitan philosopher par
excellence, perpetually in search of sensations and constantly
giving expression, or the closest thing to it, to the sensualities he
encounters. This sensuality is not only sought out in Lingis's
travel, it operates as a condition of possibility in his philosophy.
Speaking boldly we might call him a transcendental phenomenologist of sensuality. A permanent itinerant, perhaps Lingis is
one of the nomads that Deleuze and Guattari speak so fondly
about. It is rumored that Deleuze was a secret admirer of Lingis,
and it is not difficult to see why, whether true or not.[5] He is a
phenomenologist of the sensitive body, the materiality of subjectivity, and the disarming effects of travel. Focusing on a few of
Lingis's properly philosophical texts we will here examine the
constitutive role of sensation, affect, and sensuality[6] in his
conception of embodiment.

Lingis has always operated from within the phenomenological movement, tarrying with Heidegger, Merleau-Ponty, and

Levinas especially. Kant, Nietzsche, Freud, Bataille, and Deleuze are likewise familiar company. He is very close to each one of these thinkers and his writing often moves into a region of indiscernibility when he is explicating their thought. But he is no mere commentator. Woven into his strictly philosophical fabric are the faces, desires, lusts, fetishes, drives, and emotions of the innumerable others in which he has immersed himself. Photographs of these others inaugurate his chapters, capturing in a glance what takes pages to describe. His original work flows from his affective immersions, and in this way we might also call him a radical empiricist, if we mean by this that his philosophy takes seriously the plurality constitutive of sensibility and refuses to sacrifice the infinity of sensuous relations embedded in the world of experience. If Lingis breaks with his phenomenological predecessors through a re-assertion of the indelible impact of sensation on our subjectivity, it is at the same time that he is energized by a labyrinth of unknown bodies and intelligences, and the claims they have made on his body's own intelligibility. His philosophy is invested with a kind of non-philosophy, and these two modes of thought circulate through one another, creating a feedback loop of theoretical and sensuous exploitation. In short, Lingis's travel testifies to the irreducibility and immanence of the sensuous, and its role in constituting and reconstituting ourselves. A system of sensation, sensuality, and sensibility abounds in his texts and mobilizes to contest the dominance of our rationality, the fluency of our affects, and our mastery over the carnal world.

Sensation and Perception

What is a sensation? Some might classify sensation as a legend, a fantastic non-event or a dissimulation. Sensation is nothing more than a deficient mode of knowing, and thus encountered only negatively, as in Descartes. Sensation is said to be always already worked up through the perceptual or cognitive apparatus, as in

Kant. Before we know it, the idealist revolution tells us, the data of sensation have been already commandeered by our unifying faculties. We have perceptions, but can lay no real claim to sensation: they are the noumenal and the unthinkable, merely inferred. The philosophy which begins with perception or, more precisely, which champions perception's primacy, seems to have already forsaken the reality of sensation. Must phenomenology abandon sensation? Lingis believes that this is precisely what is missing from phenomenology, and thus what aligns it with idealism. In *Sensation*, Lingis declares: "Phenomenology argues that our sensations themselves are intentional; they are givens of sense, or give sense—orientation and meaning."[7] But a sensation can also be an interruption, a shift, an instigation and a disorientation. Sensations can announce the absence of sense or the onset of senselessness. A sensation can function as a kind of short-circuit of our habitual affects, our perceptual routines, our calculated taming of the environment.

For Lingis neither sensibility nor sensuality can flaunt the confident directedness of intentionality. These ambiguous passivities are basic modes of human being and enable a flexibility within the subject. Our bodies are displaced by sensations. Lingis theorizes the interruptive mode of sensation, sensation as immanently *directive*, yet without apparent meaning. By drawing a division between the representational and the affective dimensions of sensation, he allows us to distinguish between sensation as sense and sensation as affect.[8] His phenomenology of sensation unfolds into an ontology of the sensible. This is accomplished through a subtle analysis of our sensibility, one that creates a tension within the phenomenological tradition which we will have to define.

Sensation intervenes in our practice and lets slip our hold on things and on ourselves. To deny its interruptive power is to deny the subordination of consciousness to the world of corporeal experience, to assert the primacy of human access to the sensuous world which we live from. It is to pretend that the phenomenal world has never once collapsed its appearance and asserted its weight upon our bodies. Lingis's phenomenology of sensation disrupts the leveling of the world achieved in Husserl's eidetic reduction, the reduction of real objects to their phenomenal facades. It is true that the senses can be deceptive...but only to an epistemology bent on certainty.

Sensation is not first and foremost an epistemological theme. From a phenomenological standpoint which has bracketed knowledge claims, can sensation as such really be doubted or reduced? Can we *live* without sensation?

Against the grain of the phenomenological tradition Lingis maintains that we cannot fully recognize our being-in-the-world in descriptions of subjectivity that place nothingness or a hollowed-out ego at the center of our consciousness, or when the lived body is considered the vessel of an intentional consciousness that opens onto the world and moves about it with an undisturbed practical savvy (S ix). The lived body is not merely a diagrammatic entity; embodied perception is not reducible to a unified grip on the world, as though embodiment could guarantee the world will always be encountered as an intelligible whole as long as it maintains its familiar spatiotemporal coordinates. For Lingis embodiment describes first and foremost a sensual event replete with amorous and deadly—in a word, impractical—drives. We are born with forces that strive to exceed our being and we die when we are finally overcome by such forces. These are what Lingis calls the *excesses* of life. As we will see, these excesses can get caught up in circuits, or take on forms that keep them in check.

Lingis is constantly in dialogue with Merleau-Ponty's phenomenology of perception, diverging from it ever-so-slightly to make room for sensation. Merleau-Ponty goes to great lengths to exclude raw sensation from his account of perceptual experience. Perception, as intentional, is always perception-of, always the apprehension of a transcendent figure against a meaningful background. Phenomenologically this feature of perception is, in a technical sense, *given*. This background is projected by some human and ensures that the unity of things always precedes the multiplicity of their qualities. Perception structures sense-experience and staves off the immediacy of sensation with *Gestalten*. The "prejudice of sensation" gives way in Merleau-Ponty's description to the immediacy of the meaningful whole: "henceforth the immediate is no longer the impression, the object which is one with the subject, but the meaning, the structure, the spontaneous arrangement of parts."[9] The *Phenomenology of Perception* is a work that traces the minutiae of perception, and above all champions the object/horizon structure of our intentional experience. In it, an always intelligible form stages our interaction with the world.

The critique of what William James would call atomistic sensationalism is carried out by Merleau-Ponty in his defense of a desubstantialized subject, a subject fundamentally "conceived as an intentionality, a self-transcending movement of *ex*-istence, and no longer as the place of inscription of impressions."[10] Our most elementary experiences are always already meaning-laden, figural, given to us as a thing that we can get our hands around. Merleau-Ponty insists on the continuous, ordered, and horizonal structure of the stream of consciousness. What Merleau-Ponty calls the "horizon" of consciousness James refers to as "fringe." The fringe is comprised of the sets of physical and phenomenal relations surrounding any particular act of consciousness, any specific conscious state.[11] It accompanies but does not constitute the form of sensory experience. For James these relations are derived from the physiology of the body-brain schema. They constitute, in addition to the objects they involve, what Lingis would call one "level" of the world. Merleau-Ponty, by contrast, has to consider relations from the standpoint of the non-physical and non-ideal structures of consciousness. Objects and relations are seen as real only insofar as they make sense or appear within a subjective horizon. Thus, for him, relations remain at the phenomenal object/horizon level instead of opening up their own discrete sensuous dimension. Relations for Merleau-Ponty, and most other phenomenologists, are substantialized in the act of perception, but at the expense of their material substantiality. It is not the physiology of the body that apprehends objects and their relations, but the intentional structure of a desubstantialized sensory-motor schema. Here we glimpse Merleau-Ponty's idealism. But we also begin to see where Lingis situates himself, working out a middle path between the physiology of fringes and the phenomenology of perception. This eventually brings him into proximity with Deleuze via Levinas.

Is it possible to reconcile the phenomenological account of subjectivity, along with the critique of sensationalism carried out by James and Merleau-Ponty, with a realism of sensation? What if sensation could be shown to be the hinge upon which reality swings, but somehow outside, while at the same time constitutive of, experience? Kant made sensory input a transcendental condition of human experience by noting the emptiness of the categories in themselves, but at the end of the day he cognized sensation right out of the experiential world. At best sensation, insofar as it is said to derive from the thing-in-itself, is put into a precarious position, and it behooves us to remain agnostic about its reality. Lingis, by contrast, reminds us that "to sense something is to be sensitive to something, to feel a contact with it, to be affected by it" (PE 59). He proceeds to provide evidence for sensation by highlighting our passivity vis-à-vis sensory input. Sensation is not simply a stimulus given to and understood by our sensory-nervous system. It is also an exterior force that reminds us of how we are situated against our will in a sensible field of elements that leaves us susceptible to the elements. As subjects we are not only cognizant beings, but incarnated in a sensuous, preformed, and sometimes hostile world. Vulnerable and exposed, the "level of sensation *would be* the original locus of openness upon things, or contact with them" (PE 59, italics added). Before it is contoured, before it is ordered and subjected to human cognition, the phenomenological field is a sensible material set to charge the sensuality of the subject via the body's sensibility.

Lingis credits Merleau-Ponty's later work *The Visible and the Invisible* for having evaded the idealist trappings of Kantianism and modern epistemology. Actually, Lingis tells us, already in *Phenomenology of Perception* Merleau-Ponty sought to extricate himself from idealism through the complementary notions of lived body, motility, and the corporeal schema (PE 62). Against the classical accounts the subject is re-substantialized, re-sensitized[12] and given back to the sensuous medium by Merleau-Ponty's conceptual framework. With Merleau-Ponty the synthesis of experience is enacted not by the incorporeal medium of pure reason, but by the mobile perceptual schema that is incarnate consciousness. Against the twin pillars of modern epistemology, intellectualism and empiricism, he writes in *The Primacy of Perception* that embodied perception carries out a "practical synthesis" and "reveals another modality which is neither the ideal and necessary being of geometry nor the simple sensory event."[13] He continues: "This subject, which takes a point of view, is my body as the field of perception and action [*pratique*]—in so far as my gestures have a certain reach and circumscribe as my domain the whole group of objects familiar to me."[14] Supplementing Merleau-Ponty slightly, Lingis identifies this medium and its population of things as a material nexus of sensuality and sensuous objects. It is the very materiality of beings, ourselves included, which enables sensuous interaction and allows Merleau-Ponty to move toward the notion of flesh and speak of it as the folding back on itself of being (PE 62-63).[15]

The folding of the subject into the sensuality of being is what

Lingis, following Levinas, calls "involution." The substance of subjectivity is produced from out of the field of desires, pleasures, and affections accumulated within the sensual matrix. "Sensuality is a movement of involution in a medium."[16] The ontogenesis of the subject is carried out by this non-intentional, non-objective, non-attributive movement. First-person talk of "my domain" and "familiar objects" (Merleau-Ponty) loses its stability when subjectivity is conceived in this way. The subject must now be thought in terms of its original affectivity and sensation has to be seen as an immanent modification of being, an impression that moves or orders the flesh—mine, yours, ours together. Lingis shifts attention away from the invisibility of the flesh, attributed to it by Merleau-Ponty, and toward the more tangible flesh of the elemental. This has the effect of placing both the visible and the invisible on an equal plane, ontologically speaking. Lingis writes:

> The sensible flesh can be a locus where all schemes and movements of things can be captured, not because it is a blank slate or hollow of nothingness and thus a pure receptivity, but because it already contains all that the visible, the tangible, the audible is capable of, being visible, tangible, and audible itself. Itself a field where the sensible radiates and schematizes itself, it captures the patterns the exterior things emit on the variations or frequency modulations of its own body schema. (PE 63)

The subject in Merleau-Ponty finds itself caught up in the sensible world, the subject-object dialogue,[17] and a kind of corporeal grammar that organizes the lived body and inscribes its corporeity with sense. This still leaves the subject in control of itself and with a certain degree of unimpeachable practical knowledge, what Lingis identifies as "praktognosis." Despite the carnal metaphor and its connotation of the immanence of subject and world, Lingis feels that Merleau-Ponty's notion of the flesh really tames sensation by insisting on its mediation by the intentional structure of perception. Perception, Lingis contends, is derived from the sensible: "The continuity of the visible field of the world and the visible flesh itself is not itself something perceived or effected through perception, it is what makes perception possible" (PE 69). It seems that sensation must remain subordinate to perception in Merleau-Ponty's phenomenology. Just as with Kant, the phenomenology of perception relegates sensation to the imperceptible outside, thus setting it at a distance too far to cross. This is not to say that Lingis affirms our knowledge of raw sensation, but that his metaphysics prioritizes sensation while his phenomenology demonstrates our intimacy with the sensible.

What Lingis seeks to reintroduce into phenomenological description is the surplus of sensation that acts as a transcendental condition of perceptual life. This surplus he will sometimes identify as sensuality, and at other times the voluptuous or affectivity. In turn, he asserts the disruptive, or what he calls the *imperative* force, of sensuous/sensual being. Here we catch sight of Lingis's debt to Levinasian metaphysics. The sensual, for Lingis, is not something about which we must remain silent, an underlying "I know not what." Our sensibility reveals the sensual to us through its affective character: the often unbearable weight of being or the unsurpassed pleasure of existence is foisted upon us as a condition of our remaining alive in the world. To live is to be affected by the material imposition of existence, to feel ourselves engulfed in the plenitude of the world's flesh, which is nothing other than our own fleshy substance. As Lingis writes in *Phenomenological Explanations*, "to sense is to sense the substantial" (PE 67). Our subjection to sensuality is the original modality of our subjectivity (PE 69).

Material Subjects, Sensitive Bodies

Modern versions of subjectivity consistently refer to the idea that subjectivity is the aspect of human being which gathers and unifies, masters and orders the continuous series of sensations, perceptions, thoughts, emotions, decisions, and actions each one of us undergoes. This is the cogito of Descartes as well as its many variations, most of which tarry with a variation of idealism that puts a premium on human access to the world. (This does not seem to be the case with the Spinozist subject; Spinoza is a stark exception to this rule.)[18] In Kant the "I think" that denotes the purest form of the rational subject is both the transcendental and transcendent condition of any possible human experience. The multiplicity that is the sensuous world, which stands at an irreducible distance from the Kantian ego, is brought to its only manifestation by the synthesis effected by the apperceptive self. For Kant the world as I know it is my world because it is synthesized by me; the power of this synthesis is the work of the understanding and of judgment. The manifold of sensation is always already understood by the self. If it were not so, experience would crumble and the self would lose its hold on the world. Indeed, the world would fall into oblivion.[19]

The embodied consciousness we find in Lingis resists Kantian unity by remaining in contact with the multiplicity of sensuous material. Although Lingis never mentions it, his phenomenology follows in the footsteps of a fellow American, William James. It is instructive to read them together. James is rightly considered a forerunner of Husserl and a phenomenologist in his own right. He, like Lingis, fiercely resists the reduction of the sensuous and preserves its vivacity in a luscious prose rarely matched in academic writing. James is a philosopher of immanent (which is not to say immediate) sensations, a radical empiricist whose work is very much in the Bergsonian vein. (James was more than a decade older than Bergson, but their work was mutually inspiring.) Lingis shares James's flare for colorful prose, the plurality of experience, and the abundance of empirical life. Both of them could be considered "vitalists," albeit of different species. Above all, both James and Lingis insist on the unfathomable *levels*—the edges, lines, angles, hues, and planes that partition the world into unexplored and perhaps impregnable enclaves and passages—of sensible experience.[20] Together they form the seeds of an American philosophical tradition which has yet to be classified.

Lingis and James share a common critique of the Kantian subject. James distinguishes between two selves, one corporeal (the "me") and the other immaterial (the "I").[21] These two selves correspond roughly to the empirical and transcendental subjects in Kant, respectively. In his *Psychology*, James gives a shorthand account of the pure Kantian ego and calls it simply the "combining medium." To apperceive and synthesize is the "chief function" of the immaterial I. The function of the I is to organize into a neat totality the multiplicity that is sense-experience. James writes: "Without this feature of a medium or vehicle, the notion of combination has no sense."[22] For James it is the fluid stream of consciousness that unifies its successive states. Rationally organized states of consciousness are produced as convergences at the end of the stream with the help of physiological and unconscious processes, but the stream remains primary. This is why James cannot be said to follow in the wake of Kant, who must subordinate the influx of sensory data to the categories of the understanding.

Where James breaks with Kant is also where Lingis departs from the idealist strain in Merleau-Ponty. What allows James's empiricism to evade the Kantian critique of ordinary empiricism (Hume's empiricism) is precisely what Deleuze will find, ironically, so valuable about Hume—his attribution of an *immanent* transcendental ("radical") character to objective sensation. For James this amounts to the rejection of a psychologized associationism, and a positing of the objective reality of relations between material things, the pure plurality of sensuous experience, and an uncompromising resistance to the holistic tendencies of rationalism.[23] Similarly in Lingis the immanence of sensation is shown to condition the practically competent organization of the world, which is mistakenly believed to be the product of the transcendent structure of perception (Merleau-Ponty) or cognition (Kant and Hegel). Whatever empiricism is alive in Kant and Merleau-Ponty, it is not radical enough for James and Lingis.

It is not just the substantive states that build up consciousness, according to James. The transitive states are equally constitutive of subjective experience.[24] He says, moreover, that the conjunctive relations entered into by the conscious subject are affective in character, grounded in "a feeling of *and*, a feeling of *if*, a feeling of *but*, and a feeling of *by*, quite as readily as we say a feeling of *blue* or a feeling of *cold*."[25] These feelings are, for the most part, harbored in the "material me," or the body and its corporeal relations.[26] James advances a theory of corporeal grammar, or embodied significance, that is not without its analogues in the diacritical systems of twentieth-century structuralism. But his is not a theory of the subject as sociocultural function, but as materially modified or produced by bodily relations. Lingis, following James, will call the ungraspable, sensuous elements in which we move "free-floating adjectives" (I 14) so as to express the "grammatical" nature of our embodiment. None of this reduces human subjects to articulations within a discursive chain. It testifies to the fact that our bodies are sensitive to other bodies, that the conjunction and disjunction of bodies is *felt*, as well as perceived and enunciated.

As Lingis sees it, its synthetic function is not the basic function of the ego. At the least he sees the synthetic function as conditioned, not as spontaneous. James's stream seems to be equally contingent and unruly. This is partly because both thinkers are so close to the phenomenology of perception, and the specifically corporeal form given to it by Merleau-Ponty. As Renaud Barbaras has argued, any philosophy of perception worth its salt is going to have to begin its analysis of subjectivity with perception, and resist the temptation to subsume this capacity under the categories of rational thought. What we call a sensible intuition—which is nothing less than a perceptual encounter with the world—is the first revelation of an ego or self. This means, for the philosophy of perception, that apperception must conform to perception, not the other way around.[27]

The ego is not first and foremost an imprisoned and untouchable abstraction under which all experience is indexed. Nor is it merely a discursive construct, a placeholder "in the grammar of kinship, economic, and political codes." It is a naked, exposed sensuality. It is a material body invested with energy and pleasure and lust and bliss. Vulnerably exposed, it is true, but writhing with joy beneath its bare skin (I 18). Immersed in the elements the ego is fundamentally a sensuous element itself, wrapped in sensuality, "a movement of involution that intensifies and releases its energies into the elements in which the sensual body is immersed." The elements comprise the vague, ungraspable sensuous medium of nascent life—sonority, luminosity, terrestriality. As Lingis exclaims: "How calm the dawn is! How fresh it feels! How pungent it smells!—the zest and the savor vitalizing one's spiraling sensuality are cast forth again indefinitely into the depths of the dawn" (I 19). The subject stripped down is a bare enjoyment of the depths, of the countless levels of unfounded sensations.

Like James and Deleuze, Lingis advocates a form of transcendental empiricism that gives ontological priority to the role of pre-personal sensibility and corporeality in the constitution of our experience, thus making bodily sensation a condition of possibility of rationality, rational discourse, and epistemology generally. This follows Erwin Straus's *The Primary World of Senses*, in which he writes:

> Sensing is not ruled by the 'I think' which, according to Kant, must accompany all apperception. In sensing, nothing is apperceived. The sensing being, the animal, does not confront its world as a thinking being, but is, rather, related to it simply in uniting and separating.[28]

There is a type of intelligibility nascent in sensibility, an intelligibility that is affective before it is intelligible and vital before it is rational. We might call this, following Straus, an alingual animal intelligibility. It is a pre-rational intelligence that we humans share with the other fleshy beings. We, as human-animal subjects, are already subjected to a sensuous medium that preempts the judgments and rational discourses we have either invented or acquired in order to master this medium and attempt to break off from the animal kingdom.

The circuit of rational discourse which is developed and deployed, the technological and sociocultural manufacture that we toil over to wrest ourselves free from the demands of our biological composition, and the community of modern individuals that each one of us is born into—all of this is preempted by our encounter with other bodies, intruder or seducer bodies, and the appeals they make on our own. This singular community of sustenance and separation is a community which is marked by the exposure of oneself to another in the sensuous medium. My flesh is nothing other than your flesh. But my body is at the same time *exposed* to your body, the body of some animal, and the totality of objects which are folded into the levels of the world. These levels allow Lingis's phenomenology of sensation to avoid the kind of holism that would eliminate separation and freeze every entity in an undifferentiated plenum. Phenomenologically speaking, we know this is not our state of affairs. Our discrete bodies commune through a labyrinthine carnality that holds us apart at the same time that we impress ourselves upon one another, modifying the totality of the sensuous substance. Lingis writes:

> The exposed surfaces of the other do not position themselves before one as so much data for one's interpretation or as so much amorphous matter for one to give form and significance to. The carnal breaks through, collapsing the distances across which its presence can be represented. Carnal surfaces expose themselves without offering possibilities to one's powers. [...] In the immediacy of their presence, they are irremediably exterior: the surface of a sensibility, a susceptibility, a pleasure, and a torment that is irremediably alien to one and exposes a vulnerability and an alien mortality that summons one.[29]

The difference between you and I is not negligible because it is immanent, because our carnality unites us. Something of *you* always exceeds my representation of you. Alterity, however, must operate within the immanence of the sensuous element; a pure immanence traverses the merely perceived gap between I and other (S 80). Lingis has replaced Levinas's radical otherness with a radical immanence, but without giving up the exigencies of responsibility. The problem of the ethical meaning of immanent alterity emerges in Lingis's reconfiguration of the imperative.

Sustenance and Fatigue

The always antecedent presence of the material other, along with the desire or disgust it inspires in the constitution of my subjectivity, structures the ethical content of Levinas's philosophy. Lingis takes up Levinas's project, the phenomenology of the face/other, under the banner of a Kantian notion: the *imperative*. Lingis's imperative is a responsibility laid upon us by our very existence, our simple being-in-the-world. Not because we are situated among other rational beings that demand our respect, but because we could not coordinate ourselves without the stimulation of others (rational and non-rational), we are bound by an imperative. For Lingis the imperative denotes our inability to fend off sensations, our defenselessness in the face of things, other persons and animals, and the assault their earnest reality aims at us. The imperative lays claim to us as responsible agents because we are composed of the substance—the elements—of the material world. No naturalistic fallacy is committed here. Just the opposite. Lingis shows how the *is* of existence is derived from its *ought*; that is, we exist because our bodies *must* respond to a barrage of directives offering to sustain and/or diminish our vitality. Either way we must respond to these directives called sensations. Straus puts it in the following terms: "Although sensations do not resemble the things which touch us, although they are only signs of the existence of external objects, they can, nevertheless, be directional signs—that is, signs by which the other, the world, discloses itself."[30]

As world-disclosing sensations pain and pleasure indicate the presence of danger or the absence of need. What we call our freedom, our independence, our autonomy is not a brute fact or a natural given. It is gained. It is a significant mode of being, a course prescribed to us by our senses and by the sensations upon which we feed. The singularity of our lives is delineated, says Levinas, by the nourishment we enjoy in living from the offerings of life. "Enjoyment," he says, "is a withdrawal into oneself, an involution. What is termed an affective state does not have the dull monotony of a state, but is a vibrant exaltation in which dawns the self."[31] The alterity that we find ourselves thrown into, energized by, worn out by, is what gives us life and sustains us in our striving. It individuates us from the rest of our corporeal community, makes us the subjects we are. Before we can become weak, tired, or wounded we must thrive or suffer at the hands of life in the light, the earth, the air.

For both Levinas and Lingis the elemental world provides a

transcendental condition for sustenance, and thus for selfhood. The elements are our freedom (I 22). "Life lives on sensation; the elements are a nourishing medium" (I 17). The phenomenology of sensuous existence becomes here an ontology[32] of corporeal, elemental, sensual subjectivity. Lingis writes:

> Levinas's phenomenological exposition shows that prior to the anxious taking hold on things which for Heidegger makes our sensibility practical from the first, there is the contact with the sensuous medium, there is sensuality. We find things, we find ourselves, in the light, in air, on terra firma, in color, in a resonant zone. Through sensuality we find ourselves steeped in a depth before we confront surfaces and envision the profiles of objects. Sensibility opens us not upon empty space, but upon an extension without determinate frontiers, a plenum of free-floating qualities without substrates and enclosures, upon luminosity, elasticity, vibrancy, savor. (S 80)

Against Merleau-Ponty Lingis asserts that the perception of objects always occurs from out of a sensual state. Sensuality becomes the fertile ground of being-in-the-world. If Lingis breaks with Levinas, it is over the issue of the reality of objects. Although he affirms the primacy of sensuality, and, in a sense, considers contours and edges to be derivative, Lingis is not willing to efface the reality of defined and determinate objects. This would land him in a modified Kantianism that he wants to avoid. Graham Harman has shown in *Guerrilla Metaphysics* that Lingis toes the line between himself and the whole phenomenological tradition by affirming the autonomy of objects. Where for Levinas the reality of things is overshadowed by the "human hypostatization" of them, Lingis wields a realism that treats objects—and, by consequence, their sensible emissions—as the individual substances that they are. Harman writes: "The autonomy of stars and coral reefs is *real* for Lingis, no less than the independence of electric eels, cinemas, sunflower fields, snowflakes, and molten ores buried deep in the moon."[33] The countless objects and levels of the world are not dependent on us for their sensual energy, they offer themselves as so many avenues of pleasure that go about their business even when humanity is nowhere in sight.

The elements that give life to each one of us by offering themselves as the very stuff of our existence are sensuous material—luminosity, tactility, and sonority bathe our sensitive bodies. As the real source of our nourishment, they *lend us* sensibility and illuminate our world. Through the elements the affective quality of sensuality—the unbearable or ethereal modes of bare life—is able to condition our "spontaneity." No one can spontaneously wrest their psyche from a depressive state or truly induce a rapturous joy within themselves without the influence of some external power. Sensibility is not formal in its pure state, as Kant thinks. It does not come from inside and project itself outward; it does not derive from some transcendent location, over and beyond the sensuous manifold. The perceived sensuous manifold is always immersed within a sensuality which generates a creature whose sensibility emerges with its ripening.

Lingis sees sensibility as consubstantial with death. "In savoring the materiality of things sensibility has the taste of its own mortality" (S 81). Here sensibility is not just a nutritive faculty, but is also a conduit for degeneration, precisely because it is contingent. In old age sensibility yields to impairment and senility: "It is the clay of our own body, dust that shall return to dust, that knows the earth and knows itself as terrestrial. It is the liquid crystals of our eyes that are turned to the stars as to eyes of the night" (I 63). It is the liquidity of our eyes that becomes murky and prevents us from fixing upon the stars, even when they continue to shimmer. We are mortal subjects, not inviolable egos. We move our bodies throughout the world, initiating movement and automatically expending the energy we accumulate from the substance of existence. This is our burden; the source of our fatigue is living as such. Corporeity weighs upon us as the obligation to continue living.[34]

Over time we catch sight of our own degeneration. The substance that we are begins to give way, returning itself to the elements that gave it movement. Heidegger says that we exist ecstatically, always bursting forth in our temporality. Lingis reminds us that it is this same temporality, and our inability to master our own passing, that both rejuvenates and enervates our material substance. This failure is no merely ontic contingency, as Heidegger would say. In *Deathbound Subjectivity* Lingis clarifies the ontological value of our mortal substance: "The inability to put oneself back at one's beginning, to find oneself once again at the commencement of one's initiatives, to recuperate and re-present again what one had begun, which is the inner diagram of the fatigue in effort, is, across time, the condition of a subject that forms by aging."[35] That my body deteriorates against my will; that play can only be sustained for so long; because I imagine my dead body and it is as such unrecognizable as my body: my self is an other, a foreign body, for me. This other is disclosed in the world of sensation. As I grow tired and old, the possibility of my death is simultaneously the actual deterioration of my subjectivity, the dissolution of what I have managed to bring into order or to undergo. In pain or exhaustion the world infiltrates my systems and *overwhelms* me.[36] All sensitive bodies undergo a process of disorientation and desensitization as death unravels their competency.

Plasticity: Affective Circuits, Automatism, Travel

The roots of identity can be found in the affective circuits and sensitive habits that constitute the substratum of our everyday lives. These are the generic or routine practices that we induce in ourselves by force of habit or catch on to, through a kind of behavioral citation, via popular culture, tradition, and ritual. Affective circuits are survival equipment. As children, we are especially susceptible to the influence of societal forms. The *plasticity* of our physiological systems makes us pliable, malleable in the face of external forces.[37] Even perception, says Merleau-Ponty, is physiognomic[38] and, therefore, plastic. To be composed of a plastic substance is to be susceptible to influence from the outside, but resistant enough that the integrity of subjectivity cannot be consumed by the affective excesses of existence. Of course we are threatened with destruction by forces beyond our control. But for the most part our bodies subsist in a fluctuating material whose various forms prevent the total collapse of subjectivity into brute matter. This is what it means to be a plastic subject.

Affective circuits economize our actions as well as relieve a good portion of the weight of our existence and the pain of our material immanence. Following James we can locate the basis of our behavioral habits in sensation. An affective circuit, or what James calls a habitual chain, is a series of muscular contractions correlated point by point with a series of sensations. The series is set off by some sensuous stimulus or other, a muscular contraction results and gives rise to a second sensation (and contraction), a third sensation (and contraction), and so on.[39] Affective circuits aid us in walking, eating, getting dressed, socializing, communicating, etc.—all the behaviors that are ritualized into the mundane and effortless. These rituals and routines find themselves recorded in the musculature of the body and propelled along by the banal sensations that organize our typical days. These circuits coalesce into a system that subtracts from the abundance of incoming sensations and outgoing efforts required by life. They make up the constitution of our "body's attitude"[40] and, by extension, the attitudes of culture. The body is laced with an implicit knowledge that enables our escape from brute being. In Lingis's terms:

Feelings contracted from others, passed on to others, perceptions equivalent to and interchangeable with those of any
other, thoughts which conceive but the general format of the
layout about one, sentences formulated such that they can be
passed on to anyone—make up the rigorous and consistent
enterprise of evasiveness in the face of the being that is one's
own to be. (S 82)

Our bodies are adapted to the excessive content of our corporeal
existence and streamline themselves with a habitual form that
relieves them of the overwhelming scenery of life. Our prefabri-
cated and stylized life forms prevent us from imploding in the
life of our senses or becoming slaves to our libidos. For economic
purposes our sensory-motor schema adopts shortcuts that allow
it to run on autopilot. As Bergson has aptly shown, habits link us
into the mechanisms of nature as responses to the directives laid
out by those mechanisms.[41] There is no ghostly ego orchestrating
the machinery of the body, but rather a gamut of rites, rituals,
ceremonies, secret passwords and slang, a whole social circuitry
which invests the body with an identity and regulates its sensitivity. This gives the appearance of automation and total
integration into nature or culture.

Our automatic movements, our affective regularities, our
corporeal identity—these forms are *imparted* to our bodies, so
many of which await us at birth. We are sculpted, pre-sensitized
creatures. The corporeal grammar of our culture seizes us and
inscribes our bodies as soon as (even before) we emerge from the
bodies of our mothers. A natal trauma invests the child's subjectivity with a communal form, a form—a structure, a language, a
lifestyle—that initiates the body into the stratified world and
removes for good the possibility of raw sensation. This is the
price paid for becoming master of one's own field of forces, for
giving form to the surplus of sensation that inundates us upon
entry into the world. These are our birth rites. Our bodies grow

more competent as we mature. We achieve an advanced level of praktognosis as we become more familiar with the world, its offerings, and our capacity to get along within it. (Eventually this competence begins to unravel.) In a parallel formulation Deleuze and Guattari will say of social "strata" that "they consist of giving form to matters, of imprisoning intensities or locking singularities into systems of resonance and redundancy..."[42]

Our cultures impart a form to our bodies that minimizes the dangers of our plasticity. Culture lends to us its affective circuits so as to keep us from straying too far toward the extremes of our sensuality or our sensitivity—these are malleable traits, debilitating at the same time that they are protective. Our plasticity composes a significant portion of our vulnerability. It is because our bodies are made up of an organic material whose substantiality yields to external forces of decay that we are sensitive and thereby susceptible beings. Because we yield, we can encounter. If it were not so our flesh would sense nothing. We are vulnerable not only to hostile forces, but to the mundane, habitual forms imposed on us by our everyday environment. As Lingis says, "one instinctually arranges one's life so that the tasks and the tools and the problems and the encounters will recur the same each day, one avoids the limits" (S 3). Can we, should we, ward off the excesses? Is this even our decision to make? Is the excess— *pure* sensuous material—not the necessary condition of our formal constitution?

Deleuze and Guattari exhort us to destratify, to make of ourselves a "body without organs"—to oppose our own organized existence and open ourselves to experimentation, to whatever desires may come, to a nomadic movement that cuts across the circuits of our society.[43] The body without organs is a body that is free to approach the limits, to seek out what Lingis calls those "situations and adventures in which one might be swept away with a total and totally new joy" and realize "that one could never know such joy again" (S 3). The body without organs sloughs off its economizing forms and perceptual clichés. It travels outward and into the sensuous world, forsaking its affective circuits and the efficiency of its practical competence. "A cliché," Deleuze tells us, "is a sensory-motor image of a thing."[44] Clichés keep us at an ideal distance from the thing itself, always mediating and reducing our sensuous experience to the familiar, the comfortable, the safe and sound. Clichés inhibit our fantasy space. Affective circuits, corporeal forms, habits, and clichés—each of these devices perform a subtraction from sensuality and give us the impression that we are masters of our bodies. But our bodies are fundamentally enticed, engulfed, invested, and commanded by sensations that come from outside. Our sensations are not properly our own, even if they singularize us and make specific appeals to our senses. This is the meaning of Lingis's imperative. This is what it means to live from sensation, to *be* a sensitive body traversing the earth. Travel is the means by which sensation is co-opted to contest the affective circuits that form our identity; travel unleashes our bodies' capacity to affect and be affected (Spinoza).

The concept of *travel*, taken in an extended sense, is central to Lingis's phenomenology. Lingis intends travel as a destratifying practice, a practice which bursts our world wide-open. Lingis's major theoretical book *The Imperative* is a text which develops the thesis that our sensuality, by its very nature, commands our bodies to travel, to open themselves up to foreign sensations and respond to the enticement of affects we are not equipped to assimilate into our typical circuits. Lingis's primary claim in *The Imperative* is that we are not automatons, precisely because our perceptual and sensual schemata are not hardwired into our physiology or transcendental subjectivity, but nourish themselves on the contingent elementality that we live from. Indeed, the excesses of desire are the body's own vital form of destratification, the force which combats affective and perceptual automatism with internal drive. To be caught in an affective circuit is to take on a fixed corporeal form that can be resisted with the kind of exposure that comes through travel and encounters with alien forms of life. It is the kind of contingency that an affect can reconfigure in an instant, as with the death of a friend or some other unbearable trauma. What is not contingent—but also not formal—is the excessiveness of affectivity itself: it is precisely our affectivity *as genesis*, the desire for/of travel, which exceeds our formal corporeal constitution.[45] The psychogenesis of the subject is nothing other than the sensitive body in transit. This process is no less necessary for lacking formality. Weakness, discomfort, delight, and decay are necessary constituents of our material incarnation, but constitutive features which are generated as we are nurtured by the elements and enjoy our sensual/sensuous existence. This is the meaning of Lingisian travel, a concept borne of Levinasian metaphysics.

The Imperative "shows sensibility, sensuality, and perception to be not reactions to physical causality nor adjustments to physical pressures, nor free and spontaneous impositions of order on amorphous data, but responses to directives" (I 3). These directives come from sensation itself. They are indeed sensation in all its material manifestations—the humidity of the air, the scent of perfume, a tap on the shoulder, the hungry whimper of an animal under our care. All of these phenomena make material claims on my body and my material self, even if the messages they communicate to me bear no literal resemblance to the physico-physiological basis of sensation itself, or if my cognitive machinery fails to comprehend their plea. My embodied consciousness, insofar as it is a plastic perception, remains sensitive to innumerable demands and signals.

If there is anything that Lingis asks us to take from his travels, it is a recognition of the reality of sensation and the transient constitution of sensibility. At bottom the sensuous is a perpetual invitation and disruption of our practical movements and sensorial mastery, with all of their habitual investments. Sensations we have, but they are never purely our own. They belong to a transcendental flesh—a coded, affective elementality—which unites and separates us while inducing us to movement with appeals to our sensitivity. The sensory world performs our identities for us. One day the surplus of sensation rushes in and drenches us with its strange reality. When we are seized by a debilitating pain, "we feel the world attacking and invading us," says Straus.[46] Our own bodies give out and fail where they once carried us along effortlessly. Other bodies collide with our own and penetrate through our automatism, intruding on our intentions and short-circuiting our body-systems. These are the perils and promises of travel. "The traveler feels anxiety about his personal safety," writes Lingis. "He has little confidence in a personal or institutional ethics to hold back the impulses of mass desperation. The trip there has something of the feel of an act of recklessness and bravado."[47] We are met with affects, emotions, and sensations that we are unequipped to accommodate—because we are of the same substance, the same flesh, the same carnal community. For Lingis this is a community of trust, but a trust built between those we trust without knowing or choosing. The trust of strangers.

In the end, Lingis tells us, we are a community that ultimately "has nothing in common": the sustenance which circulates between bodies does not come from heaven, but from nowhere, from the groundless nothing that sustains the earth, the elements, and the other indifferently. Unlike Levinas, who triangulates the face-to-face relation with God to leverage ethical support, Lingis locates the source of the imperative and the alimentary within our material economy. "In the substance of our competence other bodies emerge, ethereal and phantasmal— bodies that materialize forces and powers that are other than those of praktognostic competence."[48] The singular matrix of forces and passions that organize our bodies comes from

elsewhere, from beyond the world of equipment that we manip-
ulate together. It is simply anarchic, but it seizes us and sends us
reeling nonetheless. When these forces materialize, it is already
too late for us to have prepared for their coming. When these
forces dissipate, our bodies return to the anonymity of the
elements—our common community. To say that we have nothing
in common is not to say that we cannot respond to an unexpected
sensation, it is to say that we cannot hope to assimilate it before
it makes claims upon our being. It is not ours to assimilate, for it
is what nurtures assimilation in the first place.

Notes

1. A slightly different version of this chapter originally
    appeared in *Janus Head* 10, no. 1 (2007): 99-122. While it is
    explicitly on the work of Lingis, it is also representative of
    what Levinasian philosophy can become.
2. A popular, budget-friendly travel guide series written for
    backpackers and hostellers.
3. Diane Ackerman, *A Natural History of the Senses* (New York:
    Vintage, 1990).
4. Lingis's original writings have prompted the publication of a
    book of essays and interviews, *Encounters with Alphonso
    Lingis*, eds. Alexander E. Hooke and Walter W. Fuchs
    (Lanham, MD: Lexington Books, 2003). A few other articles
    on Lingis are in print in various journals, including: Simone
    Fullager, "Encountering Otherness: Embodied Affect in
    Alphonso Lingis' Travel Writing," *Tourist Studies* 1, no. 2
    (2001): 171-183; Alexander E. Hooke, "Alphonso Lingis's
    We—A Collage, Not a Collective," *diacritics* 31, no. 4 (2001):
    11-21.
5. This unconfirmed bit of academic folklore was related to me
    by one of Lingis's former students at Penn State, Graham
    Harman, via e-mail on July 20, 2006.
6. Because sensation is for Lingis always charged with an

affective and/or erotic component, whether pleasurable or painful, I will often employ the term "sensuality" in places where "sensuousness," "sensitivity," or "sensibility" could work just as well.

7. Alphonso Lingis, *Sensation: Intelligibility in Sensibility* (New York: Humanities Press, 1996), ix. Hereafter cited parenthetically as S.

8. In one of his earliest essays, "Sensation and Sentiment: On the Meaning of Immanence," Lingis begins to excavate the "equivocality" of the notion of sensation. This article acknowledges the intentional side of sensation, which he links to the transcendence of the object sensed, before unpacking the immanence of sensation, which is correlated with the affective capacity of the body. Lingis here aligns himself with a form of radical empiricism which derives from the Levinasian conception of existence as enjoyment and Michel Henry's understanding of immanence. It is this empiricism that allows us to bring Lingis together with Bergson and James. For Lingis's paper, see *Proceedings of the American Catholic Philosophical Association* 41 (1967): 69-75.

9. Maurice Merleau-Ponty, *Phenomenology of Perception*, trans. Colin Smith (London: Routledge and Kegan Paul, 1962), 58.

10. Alphonso Lingis, *Phenomenological Explanations* (Dordrecht: Martinus Nijhoff, 1986), 60. Hereafter cited as PE.

11. William James, *Psychology: The Briefer Course* (Mineola, NY: Dover, 2001), chapter 2.

12. Consider the following passage from Merleau-Ponty, *Phenomenology of Perception*, 236: "In short, my body is not only an object among all other objects, a nexus of sensible qualities among others, but an object which is *sensitive* to all the rest, which reverberates to all sounds, vibrates to all colours, and provides words with their primordial significance through the way in which it receives them."

13. Maurice Merleau-Ponty, *The Primacy of Perception and Other*

Essays, ed. James M. Edie (Evanston: Northwestern University Press, 1964), 14.

14. Merleau-Ponty, *Primacy of Perception*, 16.

15. There is a whole series of contact points which obtain between Lingis and Merleau-Ponty. They cannot be followed here, where what I have tried to do is give some sense of the tension introduced by Lingis into Merleau-Ponty's theory of corporeity, even though I feel that the similarities between these two thinkers outstrip the differences.

16. Alphonso Lingis, *The Imperative* (Bloomington: Indiana University Press, 1998), 15. Hereafter cited as I.

17. Merleau-Ponty, *Phenomenology of Perception*, 132. "The subject-object dialogue, this drawing together, by the subject, of the meaning diffused through the object, and, by the object, of the subject's intentions—a process which is physiognomic perception—arranges round the subject a world which speaks to him of himself, and gives his own thoughts their place in the world."

18. The question of the unifying rational subject is difficult to locate in Spinoza because his conception of the mind (in Book II of the *Ethics*) understands the mind as the idea of the body. This problematizes our understanding of the mind as a unifying faculty. I am reluctant to make any definitive judgments about Spinoza's relation to the sensuous world. What does seem to be the case is that, in many ways, Lingis's (and Levinas's) treatment of affectivity is traceable back to Spinoza. Lingis might be seen as reaching back beyond Kant, and pulling Spinoza to the forefront of the continental discussion. I am tempted to say that Lingis is *extremely* close to Spinoza, and it is precisely on the problem of affection that they converge.

19. Cf. Immanuel Kant, *Critique of Pure Reason*, trans. Werner S. Pluhar (Indianapolis: Hackett, 1996), §16, especially fn. 202, B134.

20. The "levels" are what Lingis calls, in *The Imperative*, the plurality of dimensions of the world. In addition to the natural objects, manufactured things, humans and other creatures typically recognized by phenomenologists, Lingis recognizes the elements, lusts, and habitats that impress upon and shelter us. The night itself is as fundamental as the figure and the horizon in Lingis's phenomenology; the night is one level upon which the world rests, a dimension that beckons us into its depths.

21. Cf. James, *Psychology*, chapter 3.

22. James, *Psychology*, 67.

23. William James, *Essays in Radical Empiricism* (Lincoln: University of Nebraska Press, 1996), 41-44. To draw this point out it is useful to compare James's position with the remarks that Deleuze makes about Hume and "transcendental empiricism" in *Pure Immanence: Essays on A Life*, trans. Anne Boyman (New York: Zone, 2001).

24. James, *Psychology*, 27.

25. James, *Psychology*, 29.

26. James, *Psychology*, 44.

27. For a concise statement of this basically ontological problem, see the first chapter of Renaud Barbaras, *Desire and Distance: Introduction to a Phenomenology of Perception*, trans. Paul B. Milan (Stanford: Stanford University Press, 2006).

28. Erwin Straus, *The Primary World of Senses: A Vindication of Sensory Experience*, trans. Jacob Needleman (London: Free Press of Glencoe, 1963), 197.

29. Alphonso Lingis, *The Community Of Those Who Have Nothing In Common* (Bloomington: Indiana University Press, 1994), 177.

30. Straus, *The Primary World of Senses*, 208.

31. Emmanuel Levinas, *Totality and Infinity*, trans. Alphonso Lingis (Pittsburgh: Duquesne University Press, 1969), 118.

32. Graham Harman has written that, "The imperative actually

has an ontological character even more than an ethical one. Its target is the dreary tendency to split the world into two mutually incompatible zones, one of them a mechanistic causal chain of objects blindly assaulting one another, and the other an arbitrary space of human freedom that imposes subjective values on a mindless grid of neutral materials." *Guerrilla Metaphysics: Phenomenology and the Carpentry of Things* (Chicago: Open Court, 2005), 62.

33. Harman, *Guerrilla Metaphysics*, 60.
34. Alphonso Lingis, *Deathbound Subjectivity* (Bloomington: Indiana University Press, 1989), 154.
35. Lingis, *Deathbound Subjectivity*, 154.
36. Straus, *The Primary World of Senses*, 208.
37. Cf. James's discussion of habit and plasticity in *Psychology*, 2. We might consider the recent attempt to synthesize neuroscience and phenomenology in the work of Bernard Andrieu as an updated version of James's idea of plasticity. Brought into contact with Lingis, Andrieu's neurophenomenology accentuates the realist/materialist line of research at play in much of Lingis's texts. See, for instance, the program outlined in Bernard Andrieu, "Brains in the Flesh: Prospects for a Neurophenomenology," *Janus Head* 9 (1), 2006: 135-155.
38. Merleau-Ponty, *Phenomenology of Perception*, 132.
39. James, *Psychology*, 7-8.
40. James, *Psychology*, 9.
41. Henri Bergson, *The Creative Mind*, trans. Mabelle L. Andison (New York: Citadel, 1974), 231.
42. Gilles Deleuze and Félix Guattari, *A Thousand Plateaus*, trans. Brian Massumi(Minneapolis: University of Minnesota Press, 1987), 40.
43. Deleuze and Guattari, *A Thousand Plateaus*, 159.
44. Gilles Deleuze, *Cinema 2: The Time-Image*, trans. Hugh Tomlinson and Robert Galeta (Minneapolis: University of Minnesota Press, 1989), 20. Our clichéd perception precisely

cuts out the surplus of sensation which is harbored in every perceptual experience. This is for practical purposes, of course. "As Bergson says, we do not perceive the thing or the image in its entirety, we always perceive less of it, we perceive only what we are interested in perceiving, or rather what it is in our interest to perceive, by virtue of our economic interests, ideological beliefs and psychological demands."

45. To understand more fully the import of this ontology of affect, which is fundamental to both Levinas and Lingis, it is helpful to contrast it with the potency/act ontology of Aristotle. Edith Wyschogrod carries out this contrast in a discussion of Levinas's notions of "enjoyment" and "living from..." in her *Emmanuel Levinas: The Problem of Ethical Meta physics* (The Hague: Martinus Nijhoff, 1974), 55. Affect is shown here to break with the telos of (human) action, which for Aristotle is basic to the very being of activity. The affect of enjoyment, by contrast, is without purpose; it is simulta-neously its own potentiality and accomplishment, an active passivity which nourishes itself and produces an excess of itself. What Aristotle lacks is the lived quality of the act itself, the excess that is not comprehended by the potency/act model. "It is precisely 'life'," says Wyschogrod, "which is absent from this picture."

46. Straus, *The Primary World of Senses*, 208.

47. Alphonso Lingis, *Trust* (Minneapolis: University of Minnesota Press, 2004), 60.

48. Alphonso Lingis, *Foreign Bodies* (New York: Routledge, 1994), 24-25.

Contemporary culture has eliminated both the concept of the public and the figure of the intellectual. Former public spaces – both physical and cultural – are now either derelict or colonized by advertising. A cretinous anti-intellectualism presides, cheerled by expensively educated hacks in the pay of multinational corporations who reassure their bored readers that there is no need to rouse themselves from their interpassive stupor. The informal censorship internalized and propagated by the cultural workers of late capitalism generates a banal conformity that the propaganda chiefs of Stalinism could only ever have dreamt of imposing. Zer0 Books knows that another kind of discourse – intellectual without being academic, popular without being populist – is not only possible: it is already flourishing, in the regions beyond the striplit malls of so-called mass media and the neurotically bureaucratic halls of the academy. Zer0 is committed to the idea of publishing as a making public of the intellectual. It is convinced that in the unthinking, blandly consensual culture in which we live, critical and engaged theoretical reflection is more important than ever before.